# SAGA

Kyle Rogan

# CONTENTS

The Bible aims to tell one story: **the story of God rescuing people back to Himself through Jesus.**

But let's be honest. The Bible can be confusing and hard to understand at times. It was put together over thousands of years by dozens of people in cultures very different from our own, using a variety of genres and writing styles...and it's not even in chronological order!

**And yet, the Bible is the primary way that God has chosen to communicate with us.**

God did this intentionally. He invites us to seek Him, and He invites us to seek Him sincerely. The Bible is clear and understandable, though getting there might not be natural at times. So it's on us to step up to the plate, ask the Holy Spirit for help, and engage with God's Word.

This study is for those who...

*...wish to grow in their relationship with God*
*...feel intimidated reading the Bible, especially the Old Testament*
*...want to understand the story, themes, and people of the Bible*
*...want a resource to disciple others, be it one-on-one or in a small group*
*...want to see the connections between the Old and New Testament*
*...want to learn how to "apply" the Old Testament to their lives*

The **BEST** way to learn God's Word is with others. I *strongly* recommend finding a few friends, a mentor, or a parent to do this study with.

*SAGA* is both a Bible study and a devotional through the 12 Eras of Scripture (in other words, chronologically). Each era can be understood as a period of time or "chapter" of God's great story.

Now your Bible won't be arranged by these eras or even chronologically for that matter. This organization is simply meant to serve as a tool to understand the overall flow of the story God is telling.

Below is a short summary of each of these eras.

### BEGINNINGS ERA

God creates everything and initiates a special relationship with mankind, but mankind rebels against Him, launching the world into chaos and darkness.

### PATRIARCH ERA

God initiates a special relationship with a dysfunctional family, promising to use them in a key role in His plan to redeem the world.

### EXODUS ERA

God delivers a nation out of slavery, calling them to be His people and a shining beacon of hope to a dark world.

### CONQUEST ERA

God fulfills a promise to a friend by giving his descendants land, intending it to be His base of operations towards redeeming the world.

## JUDGES ERA

God sends leaders to help His people get back on track as they spiral out of control.

## KINGS ERA

God establishes a royal throne that is destined to rule forever, but the stability of the kingdom is shaken by unfaithful rulers.

## EXILE ERA

God exiles His people in judgment of their betrayal.

## RETURN ERA

God restores His people to their land in eager anticipation for the coming King.

## SILENT ERA

God works quietly in the background of human history as He orchestrates the next stage of His redemptive plan.

## GOSPEL ERA

In the ultimate act of love, God pays the price for humanity's rebellion and paves the way for humanity to become new creations.

## CHURCH ERA

God fills His followers with His presence, empowering them to advance His Kingdom and provide hope for the world.

## END TIMES ERA

God destroys evil once and for all and dwells fully with His people in a world greater than anything ever imagined.

This book will cover the first four eras: **Beginnings, Patriarch, Exodus, and Conquest.**

## SETTING

This is a time for you (and ideally a few others) to learn and connect with God. If you are walking through this study with others, it's up to you to decide whether you want to read a chapter together, go through it on your own first, or do some sort of hybrid. It depends on the group.

Either way, I *highly* recommend finding a special place to have this time. For one-on-one times with God, I often sit in a big leather recliner in my living room underneath a lamp with a table for my coffee. It's like my meeting place with God that helps set the tone for our time together. (I also light candles sometimes for the smell and vibe.)

Even if you're doing this study in a group setting, find a location that feels different than your normal rhythm if you can. In college, one of my best friends and I would walk down to the campus cafeteria to the same table by a large window. We also met pretty early while most other students were still asleep, so the room was relatively quiet and had few distractions. It quickly became our spot to connect with God together.

So whether you are doing this study alone or in a group, really consider your setting.

Before I begin my time with Him, I like to take a few moments to turn my phone off, breathe, and quiet my mind. I like to remember that I am sitting with the God of the universe and my Best Friend. It reminds me that He's actually present with me at that moment. If you're doing this study with others, maybe set a 30-second timer to sit in silence and dwell on the same things.

## FORMAT

Every chapter will start with an **OPENING PRAYER**. I recommend praying it out loud. For me, it helps me remember I'm talking to a real person and not just swimming in my own thoughts. It may feel awkward at first, but trust me, it'll become more natural the more you do it. The prayers in this study are snapshots of how I personally talk to God.

Every chapter will have at least one passage of **SCRIPTURE** to read that progresses chronologically through the story of the Bible. There may sometimes be additional passages that comment on the main storyline. Most of the time, I will connect a New Testament passage with an Old Testament one so we can consistently be brought back to Jesus. The whole book *is* about Him after all!

After that, there will be a list of things to **THINK** about. Every chapter will at least ask, *"Where is His grace?"* and *"Where is His lordship?"* "Grace" can be understood as love, mercy, generosity, or blessing, while for "lordship," you can think of power, authority, sovereignty, or kingship.

My hope is that this trains you to find God's character in every passage we read. Feel free to write down your thoughts or just let them swim in your head.

I will then share my thoughts and point out different ideas in the **READ** sections. But hear me on this...

**God's Word is WAY WAY WAY  WAY WAY WAY WAY WAY WAY WAY WAY WAY WAY WAY WAY WAY WAY WAY WAY WAY WAY WAY WAY  times infinity...more important and powerful than mine.**

If you sense the Holy Spirit telling you just to read the Bible and skip my thoughts, please do it! Hopefully, God will use whatever wisdom He's given me for your benefit, **but if you have to choose between reading the passage and my thoughts...pick the passage every time.**

Also, as a head's up, my Scripture quotations will be from the English Standard Version (ESV). It's just a personal preference of mine. (For more on Bible translations, check out Appendix I.)

Towards the end of every study is a list of **JOURNAL** prompts for introspection and application. These can also serve as discussion prompts with others (though some may feel better to do privately at first). Don't feel like you need to answer *every* question. I intentionally tried to include a lot of questions knowing that some will prompt better conversations than others depending on the setting or what God is trying to teach you. Some you might want to sit with longer than others, and that's okay.

These questions are meant to prompt intimacy between you and God as well as with other Christians. If going through *all* of the questions becomes more of a task than a joy, then don't.

These questions are also meant to encourage, challenge, and provide a way for the Holy Spirit to convict you. They are never meant to condemn. If you are consistently feeling condemned while going through them, take a break from them. Spend time meditating on Romans 8:1,

*"There is therefore now no condemnation for those who are in Christ Jesus."* Then go back to them when you are ready.

I also *highly recommend* getting a journal and writing things down, even if it's not your favorite thing to do. Writing helps things stick more and will remind you of your thoughts when discussing with others. It also tracks how you're growing so you can look back and be encouraged by what the Lord has been doing in your life.

This is one of the reasons why I don't leave spaces in this study for you to answer questions. This isn't meant to be a textbook for you to fill out answers. It's intended to prompt conversations between you, God, and others.

If possible, get a journal you'd really like writing in that fits your personality. It will encourage you to use it. I used composition notebooks for years but recently transitioned to some nicer leather-bound journals. Their unique texture in my hands makes my times with Him feel more real somehow, like I'm journaling my adventures with God. Call me crazy, but those little details of how you set up your time with the Lord can be a subtle game-changer.

The end of every study will have a **CLOSING PRAYER** that I again encourage you to do out loud.

Let me say this: Don't feel obligated to complete each chapter in one sitting. Some passages are longer than others, so letting the Scripture sink in by itself may be necessary. Or maybe you'll want to go slowly through the various Journal responses throughout the week. Give every chapter at least one to three days to get through.

2 Timothy 3:16-17 says, *"All Scripture is breathed out by God and profitable for teaching, for reproof, for correction, and for training in righteousness, that the man of God may be complete, equipped for every good work."*

Paul makes it clear that *all* Scripture is good for us to study and *none* should be ignored. It does pain me that we will skip some passages in this study. Here are two of the reasons why:

1) This study could quickly become overwhelming if it was on *everything* in the Bible, so I wanted to keep it manageable, mainly focusing on key stories and themes. In the future, I may branch out and do a "sub-series" on stories we skip.

2) If the whole Bible was a movie, it'd be rated "R," and I wanted to keep in mind my younger audiences and families for this particular study. Some passages are pretty intense and better learned at an older age or with a parental figure. Life is very messy and screwed up at times, and the Bible is very honest about it. We don't have to be afraid of that. We just need to be humble enough to recognize there are different times to learn different things.

Another thing: you will notice that I've capitalized pronouns referring to God ("He" instead of "he"). This is a personal preference that I have. I think it helps clarify things and reminds us of the weight of who we are talking about. The Bible doesn't tell us we have to do this. (In fact, in the original Hebrew, the Old Testament doesn't have any capitalization *or* punctuation for that matter!) I may at times capitalize titles as well, like "King" or "Good Shepherd," for similar reasons.

One of my hopes for this study is to demonstrate how to find depth in some of the more obscure and initially hard to understand parts of Scripture. To help with this, I've provided two appendices in the back of this book. The first provides a little more information on the Bible itself. The second is a list of questions that can spark curiosity while reading Scripture.

Lastly, I will approach every passage from one or two angles, but know that there are many angles from which to examine passages. Looking at the Bible my way is certainly not the only way to do so. Hopefully they will be helpful!

SAGA

*Sweet Lord*
*May You be magnified*
*May Your word remain*
*May all be forgotten*
*That's not helpful or of Your grace*

# THE BEGINNINGS ERA

# PART I: THE BEGINNINGS ERA

## SUMMARY

*God creates everything and initiates a special relationship with mankind, but mankind rebels against Him, launching the world into chaos and darkness.*

## THE SCRIPTURE OF THIS ERA

Genesis 1–11

## INTRODUCTION

Like any good story, this first "chapter" of the Bible sets the stage for everything to follow. It shows us the setting (earth), the hero (God), the problem (sin), the antagonists and villains (mankind and Satan), the hero's goal (redemption of humanity and all of creation), and the stakes (eternal destruction and separation from God). The rest of the Bible tells how God works to accomplish His goal.

Fittingly, the Beginnings Era marks the start of several themes throughout Scripture:

- The beginning of creation and God's relationship with us
- The first metaphors about water
- The first trees and river
- The beginning of sin and rebellion
- The beginning of God's plan to save us
- The first distinction between what is holy and unholy
- The first sacrifices
- The first marriages, fathers, brothers, and families
- The first judgment on evil
- The first cities of rebellion
- And many more!

What's amazing about this era is that the more you learn the *rest* of the Bible, the more you realize how much this era truly sets everything up that follows.

And it's from this era (namely Genesis 1–3) that we learn huge objective truths about our reality...

- *Who is God? What is He like?*
- *Where did we come from?*
- *Do we have value?*
- *What is our purpose?*
- *What is sin?*
- *Why is there evil?*
- *Is there hope?*

A large portion of the Biblical Worldview stems from how Genesis answers these questions. And in many ways, this era is a preview of the entire story to come...

- ° God creates everything.
- ° Mankind rebels.
- ° God sends a savior, inviting people to be saved.
- ° God wipes away evil.
- ° God begins a new world with the remnant of His people.

As you walk through this era of "beginnings," consider ways that Jesus is the "endings" of them. It's all about Him!

1

In the Beginning...

## OPENING PRAYER

*"Jesus, thank You. Thank You for this time together, for this study, and for the people I'm doing this with. May it be a blessing to my life and my relationship with You. I want to grow deeper with You and know You more. May You be praised and glorified in all these things. Amen."*

## SCRIPTURE

Genesis 1:1–3

## THINK

- *Where is His grace?*
- *Where is His lordship?*
- *Every great film typically has an opening scene that showcases the main character and the tone of the story, which prepares us for what we are about to watch. With this in mind, why do you think the Bible starts this way?*

## READ

*"In the beginning, God…"* Right from the beginning, the Bible tells us who this entire book is about: God! *He* is the main character, the main focus, the one in the spotlight. We are following *His* storyline, *His* mission, *His* goal, *His* journey.

A lot of times, we approach the Bible immediately thinking, *"How does this apply to me?"* And though that's necessary, it's imperative for us to know that this book doesn't revolve around you or me, but around God Himself. So in this study, we're going to be looking primarily at who God is, and from that we'll also learn about ourselves, the world, our relationships…pretty much everything else.

What's amazing is that later, God becomes human—as Jesus—so that we may know Him even more clearly (and for a bunch of other reasons that we'll get to eventually). But way later in the story, one of Jesus' twelve disciples, John, writes about Jesus. Look at how John decides to start his description of Jesus…

## SCRIPTURE

John 1:1–5 *(Note: In this passage, the "Word" stands for Jesus.)*

## THINK

- *What are some descriptions of Jesus that John gives us?*

## READ

John tells us that Jesus was there right at the beginning! Genesis 1:1–3 actually shows the Trinity: God the Father, the Holy Spirit (hovering over the waters), and Jesus (aka God's Word) speaking creation into existence.

Look at Genesis 1:26...see how God refers to Himself as "us" and "our"? This is an important reminder that the God of the Old Testament is the same God of the New Testament.

We may at times want to mentally swap in "Jesus" for "Lord" or "God" when we read Old Testament passages and vice versa in the New Testament. The same goes for the Holy Spirit. (This might not work all the time due to theological implications and the nature of God being "three in one." Consider it an exercise with limitations!)

All three persons of our one God were there together at the beginning launching the creation process. And how? By God's Word. **God's Word was all that was needed to create life. Put another way, Jesus was all that was needed to create life.**

What this means is that when we read God's Word, the Bible, with the presence of the Holy Spirit helping us, there is life spoken into us. We are letting the Creator do what He does best: create! One of the most important things we can do throughout this study is to let Christ be the One to speak to us. We must really listen, receive, submit to, and accept His Word if we want to see any impact from Him in our lives.

## JOURNAL

**Before Jesus spoke, the earth was dark, without structure, and empty.** What darkness, chaos, and emptiness are you experiencing right now, both circumstantially and internally? Don't just think about them. Write them down or say them out loud.

**Jesus speaks, and everything changes.** In those places, where would you like Jesus to speak light into the darkness? Order where there is no structure? Fullness or completion from emptiness?

**The Bible opens up with the story revolving around God.** Did your responses above revolve around His glory? Or yours? How might His interpretation of "light, structure, and fullness" differ from yours? Take some time to ask Him to change your will to be more in line with His.

**Our world is characterized by darkness, chaos, and emptiness.** You and your community, the church, are the primary ways Jesus speaks today (after the Bible). Who in your life needs you to speak "light, structure, and fullness" to them? (This could be hope, encouragement, challenge, peace, mercy, affirmation, your silent presence…) How might *they* define the "light, structure, and fullness" they need? How might God's interpretation differ/be similar? Pray for wisdom and take advantage of the opportunities He gives you this week to speak His "light, structure, and fullness" into their lives.

## CLOSING PRAYER

*"Lord, please help me live like You so I may bring Your light and life to others. May I be like You and be a person of generosity in word and deed. May I leave this time changed by You. I love You! Amen."*

2

# In His Image

## OPENING PRAYER

*"Hi, Jesus. Thank You so much for this time to spend together. Thank You for designing me to be in relationship with You from the very beginning. May these intentional times together become more and more natural and life-giving as I practice being in Your Word and in Your presence. May this time be blessed that I may be able to receive what You have for me. Amen."*

## SCRIPTURE

Genesis 1:1–2:3

## THINK

- *Where is His grace?*
- *Where is His lordship?*
- *How can we see God's character? His personality? What He's good at? What He cares about? How He does things? His goals? (Maybe set a goal for yourself to name thirty different things. They're there!)*

## READ

This opening chapter magnificently shows us a picture of who our main character is. God's power, character, and personality are on complete display. There are *so* many things we can learn about Him here, but I'm just going to point out three I've found: His use of **Process, Intentionality,** and **Authority**.

There's a lot of debate about whether these six days of creation are meant to be read literally or metaphorically. But how about the fact that God created things over the course of time at all?! He's able to create everything in one moment, but He doesn't.

Why? One reason is that's simply who He is. **He does things through a process.** He works gradually, taking His time, but He *will* complete what He set out to do.

A second thing to see is His intentionality. **God creates everything for a purpose.** Everything He makes is made for humanity to exist, thrive, reflect Him, and enjoy Him. Take a look at the passage again. See if you can find all the ways each portion of creation reflects this purpose.

Perhaps the one that blows my mind the most is in verse 14 when God makes the sun and moon. The NIV (New International Version of the Bible) says that they should *"serve as signs to mark sacred times."* Well, what sacred times will God want them to remember? One of the biggest is Passover, when God miraculously delivers His people out of slavery.

Did you catch it? Before sin even enters the world, God plans to celebrate His victory over delivering His people. Incredible.

Finally, did you catch how He gives authority to *"govern"*? Only those with authority can give authority. And **God establishes Himself**

**as the ultimate Authority.** As Creator, He assigns purpose, responsibilities, roles, relationships, laws, consequences, order, blessing, and structure. As much as we tend to buck at the idea of having someone over us, God gives us no wiggle room in this. He makes it very clear that *He* is God, and we are not.

What's amazing is that God passes on many of His attributes to us as His image-bearers. No single person can encapsulate all that He is, so He creates each of us as miniature pictures of Him, each showcasing who He is in a unique way. He is a relational God who wants to expand His goodness, glory, joy, and blessing beyond just Himself! Look at what He tells humanity to do in verses 28-30:

- *"**Be fruitful and multiply**"* Make more humans just like He did. God built a family, so we are called to build more.
- *"**fill the earth**"* God started to fill the earth with His creations, so we are called to fill the world with people, cultures, and creations of our own.
- *"**subdue it, and have dominion over**"* God subdued the chaotic "*waters*" in verse 2, so we are called to subdue the chaotic "*waters*" (nature) of the world to make it a place of peace, abundance, and order.

Only the Garden of Eden appears to be cultivated land at this time. Humanity is meant to spread throughout the world and bring order, structure, and life to the rest of it, just like God did.

Do you see how we are supposed to be miniature pictures of who God is? His design for us to be *like* Him is an inherent invitation to live *with* Him in a loving relationship. Well, in a couple of chapters, everything will go wrong and humanity will stop living like God. But then Jesus will come...

## SCRIPTURE

Colossians 1:15–20

## READ

Jesus arrives as the *perfect* image of God. He lives like we were supposed to and *with* the Father in a perfect relationship. If you want to know what God is like, look at Jesus! If you want to know what it means to live as an image-bearer, look at Jesus! Through Him, we receive new life and the gospel spreads.

And **as more people follow Jesus** (*"be fruitful and multiply"*)...
**...they tell more people about Jesus** (*"fill the earth"*)...
**...to usher in the Kingdom of Jesus** (*"subdue it, and have dominion over"*).

God calls us to be more like Jesus!

## JOURNAL

**Think about the characteristics of God you listed.** Which ones bring you the most comfort and why? Take some time to praise God concerning those things. Thank Him for how you've seen them in your life.

**Consider how God does things through a process, is intentional, and has authority.** Where have you seen this in Scripture? How about in your own life? Where do you need to submit to these truths about Him?

**Think about some of your passions and interests.** How might these things be similar to God's passions and interests? Sometimes we compartmentalize areas of our life as "this is mine" and "this is God's."

How can you instead do these things as a reflection of Him? (Remember, *He* is your role model in how you do them!)

## CLOSING PRAYER

*"God, You are so unbelievably creative and wonderful. May I live and think in a way that is honorable to You today as Your image-bearer. And may I love others as they are also. Thank You for the example of Jesus! I love You, Lord. Amen!"*

3

# The First Relationships

## OPENING PRAYER

*"Hello, Friend! Thank You for this time we get to be together today. Would You please settle down my mind and emotions so I can focus on being in Your presence at this moment? You are worth every minute. May I hear Your voice and be changed by Your word today. Amen."*

## READ

Remember how we mentioned that people have different ideas about how God created the world? Well, that conversation carries over to this chapter also, but for now you can think of the story zooming in to retell what happened in Genesis 1 from a more intimate perspective...

## SCRIPTURE

Genesis 2:4–25

## THINK

- *Where is His grace?*
- *Where is His lordship?*

*• What are some implications of God creating humanity as men and women? Why did He do it this way?*

## READ

There are a lot of conversations these days about what it means to be a man or woman. When God makes humanity, He creates them male and female in His image. *So both men and women are equal in value, worth, and dignity as rulers over the earth.* Both are designed to be His beloved sons and daughters.

Alongside this, God also made men and women differently so that they could glorify Him in unique ways. There are obvious biological differences that put God's creativity on display and allow Him to create more image-bearers through them.

And then there are more general ways men and women are different psychologically and sociologically. These are not just good things, but *very good* things in God's eyes. So we are called to glorify God in the uniqueness of how He made us, rejoicing in how He has crafted the other.

Beyond that, we are made with even more specificity. (Read Psalm 139 to see more!) Not every man is called to be exactly like every other man, and the same goes for women. Some women have different gifts and passions for athletics, arts, cooking, decorating, building, programming, engineering, leading...and the same goes for men. There's no such thing as a "cookie-cutter" Christian. God calls us to live as we are with the gifts He's given us to become clearer pictures of who He is.

In this passage, God is creating the first-ever relationship between two people: a marriage (clarified in verse 24). Not a brother and sister, not a mother and daughter, not two bros hangin' out...but a husband and wife.

It is in this paradise that, for the first time, God declares something to be "not good": Adam being alone. Even though the world was perfect, he needed a helper (think teammate, partner, or friend who's got your back).

So God brought all the animals before Adam to be named, and I believe it is during this process that Adam realized this lack God saw in his life. Each male animal had a female counterpart...where was his?

When Adam sees God bring Eve to him in verses 22–23, he exclaims in love poetry, *"This at last..."* To me, this implies that Adam had felt lack and that now God was meeting that need over abundantly.

In verse 25, we see they *"were both naked and were not ashamed."* Their marriage was a perfect friendship! They felt no embarrassment or awkwardness. There was no insecurity, fear, anxiety, or wondering if the other person loved them. They probably had fun and laughed a lot together!

In verse 24, it says they were *"one flesh."* Similar to how God is one God as Father, Son, and Holy Spirit, a married couple is one flesh as husband and wife. It's another way we are meant to be a picture of God. God cares a lot about marriage for this reason.

Our culture has mixed feelings about marriage right now. On one hand, it's seen as a bad way to lose your independence. Culture says, *"You should be able to love who you want, when you want, for however long you want."* And we end up reducing marriage to feelings that revolve completely around us.

On the other hand, sometimes our culture sees marriage as the best thing that can ever happen to you. It should solve all your problems, make you "complete," and bring you "happily ever after." Both views are incredibly wrong.

Jesus told us in Matthew 22:30 that there won't be marriage on the New Heaven and New Earth, so it's impossible for a marriage to bring "happily ever after." **Marriage is meant to be a living, temporary picture of who God is and His love for us until we are with Him in the New Heaven and Earth.**

This will be a *huge* theme in the stories ahead. The Bible begins with a marriage between Adam and Eve in Eden and ends with a marriage between Jesus and His bride (the church) in a new and better Eden (see Revelation 21:9). So, having a proper view of marriage is incredibly important to understanding God.

## JOURNAL

**God created you as the sex you are, uniquely and intentionally.** How can this truth embolden and comfort you as you navigate the voices of our culture? (This applies to some areas of "Christian" culture too!)

**You might be one of the few men/women of God that someone knows.** What is your pattern of thinking or talking about the opposite sex? Do you think little or poorly of them? Do you criticize? Judge? Belittle? Objectify? Ignore? Feel bitter towards? Feel better than or superior to? Confess anything the Lord brings to mind. Take a step this week to ask someone you trust, *"Do I honor men/women in how I behave towards them?"*

**How we see marriage impacts how our marriages will go.** If you are unmarried and desire to be married, how do you see marriage? Do you see it as something that revolves around your desires? Or a sort of "savior" for your life? How might God want to correct your view? How might you be more fulfilled and blessed by His correction?

## CLOSING PRAYER

*"Lord, please teach me how to be someone who loves people of the opposite sex well. May I honor, respect, encourage, and value them as You do me. And may I honor, respect, and value You in how I view myself. I love You, Lord. Amen."*

4

# The Fall

## OPENING PRAYER

*"Jesus, there are times when the state of the world weighs heavily on me. Please speak clearly to me so I may know how to be faithful in such dark times. I want to be a light and glorify You. Please lead me to truth. Amen."*

## SCRIPTURE

Genesis 2:16–17
Genesis 3:1–24

## THINK

- *Where is His grace?*
- *Where is His lordship?*
- *What are the tactics Satan (aka the serpent) uses to deceive Eve?*
- *What are the effects of sin we see here?*

## READ

It is here we are introduced to our first antagonist: Satan. We learn from Isaiah 14:12–14 and Revelation 12 that Satan used to be an angel who led a rebellion of a third of the angels against God to make himself like Him. But God being, you know, *God,* thwarted Satan and cast him out of heaven down to earth. These angels we now call demons.

Despite all that God did for humanity and His heart for them to have full, abundant lives, mankind decided they wanted to rule instead. And we still decide that today. Satan leads us to things that we **SEE.** We are faced with temptation every day and have the choice to obey God or not. But before Eve took the fruit, her mind changed. She **CONSIDERED IT GOOD** to eat it. It was after that that she **TOOK** action.

See, God **CONSIDERED IT NOT GOOD** for Eve to eat, but Eve decided to disagree. Her heart and mind together decided that she was a better judge of what was good and not good instead of God. In essence, she threw a coup against God's Kingdom, declaring herself queen of her own life.

And this is the root cause of *every* sin. We are faced with temptation and forced to decide between what *we* think and feel and what *God* thinks and feels. Adam and Eve both chose to follow their own hearts instead of God's heart. We will see this pattern of people following their hearts instead of God's over and over again, and it will lead to devastating consequences.

Now following your heart and thoughts won't always lead to destruction, but that's *only* if your heart and thoughts happen to be the same as God's. You've probably followed your heart and thoughts without consequences, but that's how sin sometimes works. God told Adam and Eve they would surely die if they ate from the tree, but they didn't die right away. It came slowly over time, eating away at them. This is why we need to focus on obeying God even if the consequences of our actions don't seem to exist or be that bad.

As a result of this action, **our relationship with ourselves is broken**. Adam and Eve felt shame and hid. We do the same thing. We feel embarrassed, condemned, ashamed, fearful, proud, arrogant, insecure...

**Our relationships with others are broken.** Adam and Eve were supposed to be best friends sharing everything together, and they hid from each other. We experience envy, anger, bitterness, fear, hatred, lust, jealousy...

And most importantly, **our relationship with God is broken.** He was to be our good King and ruler, but we decided that we wanted to rule ourselves. So now we naturally rebel against God. It's why most kids' shows teach lessons on how to be good. It implies that without correction, they will grow up to follow immoral impulses.

But even then, God still desires us and wants His glory to be seen in our lives. In Genesis 3:15, God promises to send an offspring of Eve to destroy Satan. It's our first foreshadowing of a coming savior. How amazing is His love! And He hints at how He will do it in verse 21...

God makes them clothes of animal skin to cover their shame. But where did the animal skin come from? An innocent animal! **God killed an unwilling, innocent animal to cover some of their shame in the garden. But Jesus is greater than that animal. He was innocent and *willing* to sacrifice *Himself* to erase *all* of our shame!**

## SCRIPTURE

Revelation 3:1–6

## READ

In this message to the church in Sardis, Jesus is challenging His people to endure for His name's sake. And to those who keep the faith (*"conquer"*), He will clothe in white robes, making them perfect and free from sin and its effects. No more self-destruction, no more barriers in relationships, and a perfect relationship with God.

And until Jesus clothes us, we are called to live as forgiven people free from shame like Adam and Eve were supposed to. Jesus is the perfect example of how to live in a broken world, and He's given us imperfect examples in the stories ahead so we can learn from their victories and mistakes.

## JOURNAL

**Jesus has declared what is good.** Has there been anything you have been "considering good" that Jesus doesn't? See if you can articulate how you progressed from SEEING to CONSIDERING IT GOOD to TAKING. Take courage and spend some time asking for forgiveness. Jesus never turns us away when we bring our shame to Him!

**Satan likes to make us think we are stuck in our shame.** If you have confessed and asked for forgiveness, spend some time reminding yourself of His love for you and that He calls you to walk away in freedom from shame with Him. Praise Him for this!

**Sin breaks relationships.** Are there any relationships in your life that are broken by shame? Bitterness? Fear? Hatred? Jealousy? Spend time confessing how you have contributed to the brokenness. Ask Him how to redeem the relationship if possible. Seek wisdom from other Christians (ideally further along in their faith than you) on what reconciliation may look like.

## CLOSING PRAYER

*"Jesus, thank You for offering Yourself as a sacrifice for my sins. Thank You for forgiving me. It's hard to feel forgiven sometimes. Please help my feelings catch up to what is true! Thank You for always being with me and never turning me away. May I be like You towards those I need to forgive. I love You, Lord!"*

5 |

## Cain & Abel

## OPENING PRAYER

*"Hello, my Friend. You are so good to me. Thank You for helping me have time today to be with You and get to know You more. These moments are so special. Please open my eyes to see that You are good and soften my heart to receive whatever it is You want me to get. I love You. Amen."*

## SCRIPTURE

Genesis 4:1–16

## THINK

- *Where is His grace?*
- *Where is His lordship?*
- *Make a list of the top ten people you are closest to. They don't need to be in order. (We'll come back to this...)*

## READ

We don't know what motivated both men to bring sacrifices to God, but there was something about Abel's sacrifice that reflected his love for

God while Cain's didn't. Later, God will set up a sacrificial system for Israel to practice, but throughout Scripture we learn that sacrifices were meant to reflect one's heart towards God.

Psalm 51:16–17 says, *"For you will not delight in sacrifice, or I would give it; you will not be pleased with a burnt offering. The sacrifices of God are a broken spirit; a broken and contrite heart, O God, you will not despise."*

God apparently *did* despise something about Cain's attitude. While Abel was experiencing the natural blessings (God's *"regard"*) that come from being in a deep relationship with God, Cain grew jealous of that favor. It seems that Cain wanted the **blessings** from God but not the **relationship** with God Himself.

Perhaps he thought that doing some "religious exercise" warranted favor from God. It'd be like saying to God, *"Why haven't You blessed me in this area of my life? Don't You see how good I'm being?"* But God delights when we come to Him just because He is who He is.

And of course God wants a great relationship with Cain...He loves Cain! So much so that He brings this issue up with Cain to help Him get back on track. *"Doing well"* or *"doing right"* naturally leads to depth with God, just like any other relationship. If you are ambivalent towards a friend, that friendship won't last much longer!

Apparently, Cain's thoughts and heart had grown bitter, angry, and jealous until eventually Cain just *followed his heart*, which was to kill Abel. Just like his parents, Cain **SAW** Abel's favor, **CONSIDERED IT GOOD** to kill him, and **TOOK** Abel's life from him.

God even warned Cain about this. See, our flesh (aka our natural inclination) is against God and towards evil. Unless we *"rule"* our hearts and minds, our sinful hearts will take over and carry us to destruction. This is why *"following your heart"* is evil advice. **God tells us not to follow our hearts, but to *rule* them.**

But Satan knows following our hearts is easier. It's what we naturally want to do after all! So he will do everything he can to encourage us to do so. See how God describes sin as *"crouching at your door"*? It's like a lion waiting for an antelope not to notice it...and then it strikes! Look at how Jesus compares Satan with Himself...

## SCRIPTURE

John 10:10–15

## READ

Satan's goals of "stealing, killing, and destroying" have always been the same since the Garden of Eden and with the same method: **deceit**. He makes things look and sound good to trick us into following our hearts instead of ruling over them as God tells us to.

So the task is to identify the lies Satan tells us and lead our hearts and minds to truth instead. But how could we do this if we are so easily deceived? Fortunately, Jesus has decided to be our Good Shepherd. Jesus is a better version of Abel.

**Where Abel was a shepherd, murdered because his brother was jealous of his sheep, Jesus is a better Shepherd who *let* Himself get murdered *for* His sheep.**

## SCRIPTURE

Psalm 23:1–4

## READ

Jesus is the one who leads us away from Satan's lies towards truth if we stay close to Him. Sometimes He will use his "rod and staff," disciplining us to get us on the right path and calling out sin in our lives so we don't go down dangerous roads. He is a Good Shepherd who wants the best for us, but only He knows the way.

Knowing this, we must keep confessing our sins to Jesus when we recognize them. And when we don't see any sin, we ask Jesus to show us just in case we are missing it! Otherwise, anger, bitterness, envy, lust, and things like that will continue to grow. Jesus is always ready and willing to help get us back on track if we let Him!

## JOURNAL

**Look at the ten people you listed earlier.** Because Satan loves division, these are the relationships he probably wants to ruin the most. So he's going to take every chance he gets to break those relationships with your sin. Have you noticed any ways he has already deceived you? Anyone you need to forgive or ask for forgiveness?

**Think back to some times when Jesus needed to correct you.** How did He do it? Circumstance? Through others? Scripture? See if you can list them. Do you see any similarities? Any patterns? Are there ways you can see Him trying to correct you now?

**Think about the people in your life over whom you have influence.** Think for a moment about the kind of advice you give them. Do you point people towards *"following their heart"* or towards Christ's desires for them? Do you focus on making them feel good, or do you try to be a mouthpiece for Jesus in that circumstance? Challenge yourself this week to slow down and really seek Christ's wisdom when advising others.

## CLOSING PRAYER

*"Jesus, thank You for stories of warning like this one. I don't want to be deceived like Cain or choose anger like he did. Please help me see my sin so it doesn't grow anymore. I am sinful and need You to lead me to goodness. Thank You, my Good Shepherd. I love You."*

6 |

# Lamech & His Sons

## OPENING PRAYER

*"Dear Lord, thank You so much for this time we get together. As I dive into this seemingly random part of the Bible, please open my eyes and ears to see and hear what You would have for me. Please lead me to truth and life. I love You so much! Amen."*

## SCRIPTURE

Genesis 4:10–24

## THINK

- *Where is His grace?*
- *Where is His lordship?*
- *How would you describe the state of humanity at this point?*

## READ

Cain the murderer now lives his life afraid of being murdered. He builds a city, possibly as a sort of self-defense. It is deeply ironic and tragic. But God in His grace and desire to curb evil's spread puts some sort of mark on Cain as a warning: Don't tempt God's wrath.

Then we meet the man who does: Lamech.

He's the first man to take *two* wives. With Adam and Eve as our example, we know that this is not what God intended (Genesis 1:24). Like Adam and Eve's sin, Lamech **SEES** the two women, **CONSIDERS THEM GOOD,** and then **TAKES** them for himself.

From this action alone, we see that Lamech treats these women not as equals to be loved and respected but as objects to acquire and make himself feel good. (Lamech was only *"following his heart"* after all...) We will see this play out tragically over and over again in the story of the Bible, and it never goes well.

Not only that, we see Lamech actually *bragging* about killing a man in verse 23 and challenging God to bring a curse worse than the one on Cain! Where God declares Cain's mark to be a warning, Lamech views it as a badge of honor.

From these two things, we see that humanity is getting worse, not better. The separation between Adam and Eve is nothing compared to Lamech and his wives. The evil of Cain's actions is nothing compared to Lamech's boastful violence. **Sin, unless it is stopped, causes things to get worse and worse, generation by generation.**

Take a look at Lamech's sons. Jabal is an animal-breeder, Jubal the first inventor of instruments, and Tubal-cain a man who builds tools. Some might say, *"Society is getting better. Look at all we're accomplishing!"* And while the accomplishments sound awesome, the more important issue is the hearts of people.

One of the intentions of tracing Lamech's line is to point out generational corruption. So why are these technological advancements included? Are animal husbandry, music, and technology bad? Of course not! If anything, they are neutral.

But think, *why* does it mention that *they* created these things? Well, what has happened? Sin! The world is now broken and now mankind is trying to fix it.

Perhaps Jubal looked at the cursed ground, which made it difficult to grow food, and decided to breed animals. Tubal-cain made tools, presumably to help till the soil for a similar reason. (We may also imply the creation of weapons for both offensive and defensive purposes.) What about music? Perhaps Jubal found music as a way to process his brokenness, as many of us do when we listen to music.

Each of them deals with the brokenness of sin in different ways. Some through greed, violence, and lust like Lamech. Some pour themselves into their work like Jabal and Tubal-cain. And others through self-expression, perhaps like Jubal did.

Today we have incredible technology at our fingertips. Yet we are filled with division, hatred, greed, racism, selfishness, pride, anxiety, depression...technological advancement hasn't solved the sin problem. This is why we can't put confidence in our accomplishments to make things better. We need some*one* else...

## SCRIPTURE

John 5:2–9

## READ

Thirty-eight years. Probably an outcast, unwanted. No relatives in sight that we know of. All he had was this pool of water. His life was consumed with getting into that water so he could finally be healed. Then, *maybe then* he could have the life he always wanted, where he could feel loved and like he actually belonged. He feels so close but can never make it...

**Then Jesus shows up, and everything changes.** *He* is the one able to give the man what he needs. **Only Christ can truly fill the lack we have in our lives.**

## JOURNAL

**Lamech placed his identity in being a "worse Cain."** It likely made him feel good about himself, confident, strong...like he knew who he was. Where do you tend to place your identity? Would you feel despair if it was taken from you? Where do you feel the things Lamech felt?

**Lamech saw his sin as "badges of honor."** Do you have any ungodly "badges of honor" like Lamech? Like how much you can hold your alcohol? How many sexual exploits you've had? How many deals you can cut at the expense of others? How much money you can store up for yourself or splurge on? How much money you can give for the wrong reasons? Do you take pride in how many "religious practices" you do during the week?

**Consider how Lamech's sons compensated for their brokenness.** Where do you go to find healing? How do you compensate? Do you splurge? Work? Create? Numb with social media or video games? Obsess over your appearance or status? Overeat or down alcohol? Spiral into mental paralysis, anxiety attacks, or self-criticism?

**Jesus wants your confidence to come from your faith in Him.** Pray over the things you listed, confessing them to Jesus and asking for victory over them in your life. He desires victory for you!

**Think about people you know who pour themselves into things other than Jesus.** Can you identify the need they are trying to fill? *Belonging, purpose, friendship, love, feeling wanted or beautiful...* What are some ways *you* can be like Christ in their life? This doesn't necessarily mean solving their problems, but it could be meeting some of their needs. Unconditional friendship is a great start!

## CLOSING PRAYER

*"Friend, it is really easy for me to pour my life into things other than You, especially when things are tough. Please help me more naturally come to You during those times. Help me bless those in need around me. Amen."*

7

# Enoch

## OPENING PRAYER

*"Dear Good Shepherd, thank You for leading me into this time together. It is good to walk with You. You lead me in peace, and You are so patient with me when I get off track. Please help me focus my thoughts on You and my desires on You. Amen."*

## SCRIPTURE

Genesis 4:25–5:27
Hebrews 11:5–6

## THINK

- *Where is His grace?*
- *Where is His lordship?*
- *What can we learn about the state of humanity?*

## READ

Hebrews 11 is often nicknamed the "Hall of Faith." It is filled with a list of imperfect, faithful men and women God used in incredible ways. And tucked away in this long list of famous people like Abraham,

Moses, and David, we get Enoch...a dude who only really shows up for a few verses in the whole Bible.

The thing about Enoch is that he *never died*. Only one other person never dies in the Bible (no spoilers). Over and over again in this genealogy, it says "[So and so] lived [so many] years, had [these kids], and then died." But not Enoch. He was simply *"no more, because God took him away"* as the NIV puts it.

So why didn't Enoch die? Why is he included in the "Hall of Faith"? Did he do some big miracle? Lead a revolution? Lead tons of people to Jesus? Display great acts of courage? Was he famous? Did he defeat armies? Did he change the world? What?! *WHAT DID HE DO?!*

He walked with God. That's all it says.

*"But that can't be it, right?"*

Jude 14–15 says he prophesied, but so did many others in Scripture, and they didn't go straight to heaven. He was simply a normal person who had a deep relationship with God.

And that's one of the big points here.

There was nothing extraordinary about Enoch in the world's eyes. **All he did was walk with God, and that was enough.**

So often we put tons of pressure on ourselves to become something great. To reach a certain level of success by a certain age. To get married and have the "perfect family." To get good grades, social praise, or a role of distinction. To change the world or make a difference. To be busy, even with "holy" things.

Think about the people we hold up as celebrities and heroes in our culture. Their social value is based on what they were able to achieve, attain, or accomplish. Without those things, they would be "no ones" like everyone else.

Having cultural heroes can be a very good thing, and the Bible is filled with heroes. **But we need to know deep down that God's love for us isn't based on what we can achieve, attain, or accomplish.**

We sometimes think, *"In order for God to love and approve of me, I need to accomplish this or that and never mess up and be absolutely perfect."* So we either suffocate ourselves with pressure or don't even try to follow Him fully.

Either way, we act out of shame for not being who *we* think we should be. We let *our own declarations* of our worth trump *God's declarations* of our worth...meaning we usurp His authority over us! We **SEE** our accomplishments, **CONSIDER THEM NOT GOOD**, and then **TAKE** action from a place of shame.

We know Enoch wasn't perfect. Only Jesus is! **So Enoch was just a regular guy who spent time with God daily and tried his best, and that was enough. Jesus was a *perfect* "walker with God," so we can look to Him as an example of how to do it!**

This is really great news! Now when we work to achieve, attain, or accomplish, we don't *need* to do it for approval. Because of Jesus, we are already wanted and desired by God! Enoch knew God loved him, so he responded in love.

So now we *get to* pursue our work with a greater purpose, working *with Him* to build His Kingdom. It's easier said than done of course, but if we practice putting our worth in what Jesus says about us and try-ing our best to walk *with* Him every day, that's enough.

## JOURNAL

**Just like when we walk with someone with a different pacing than ours, our pace can differ from God's.** Do you tend to "run ahead" of God trying to earn love and affirmation from Him by trying to be perfect? Or do you tend to "walk behind" God, so afraid of failing that you hesitate to obey Him fully? How would walking *with* God change how you do things?

**Identify times when your chest clenches up, your mind spins, you react to things impulsively, or you feel burdened with the weight of the world.** Are these moments rooted in trying to earn affec-tion, love, security, confidence, worth, value, or belonging? What truths from God can you use to combat your responses?

**Sometimes our days feel like chores.** Something we *have* to go through. Enoch probably had thousands of days like this…but God had a perspective on his life that Enoch couldn't see. His daily, regular faith-fulness through normalcy is being used at this very moment to bless us. Your faithfulness through the monotony is not wasted. *He* is using it for preparation of things to come *and* to be a testimony to those around you. Identify monotonous rhythms in your life. How can you "pour into" those rhythms that they may be more fruitful for your faith?

## CLOSING PRAYER

*"Jesus, You know my walking habits. Please show me how You walked with the Father so I can learn how to do it also. I don't want to feel pressure or shame, and I know You don't want me to either. Thank you for your patience with my pacing. I love you!"*

# 8

# Noah & the Flood

## OPENING PRAYER

*"Dear God, thank You for this time together. Thank You for seeing me, hearing my prayers, and being with me every moment of the day, even when I don't recognize it. Please help me concentrate as I delve into your Word today. I love You! Amen."*

## SCRIPTURE

Genesis 6:1–9:17

## THINK

- *Where is His grace?*
- *Where is His lordship?*
- *Think back to the creation story in Genesis 1. What are some similarities you see? What are some differences?*

## READ

Though some disagree, the oldest and most widely held interpretation of Genesis 6:1–4 is that these *"sons of God"* were fallen angels (demons) who married human women and had children with them called the Nephilim. (The phrase *"sons of God"* is used to describe spiritual beings elsewhere in the Bible, like in Job 1:6.)

Now before you panic about accidentally marrying a demon, Peter and Jude mention that these particular demons have already been *"locked away"* until the day of judgment (2 Peter 2:4; Jude 6).

You might've noticed how these demons **SAW** the daughters of man, **CONSIDERED THEM** attractive, and **TOOK** them as wives. Looks like we've discovered our inspiration to sin!

Some believe that this was part of Satan's scheme to undermine God's plan to bring a savior through the offspring of Eve. He manipulated Cain to kill Abel (perhaps thinking he was that savior), and now he's trying to compromise the very bloodline of humanity itself. If he could somehow persuade this savior to follow him instead of God, he'd win!

Fortunately, God had other plans. And regardless of whether the Nephilim were half-human, half-demon people or simply powerful, corrupt men like Lamech, **God is heartbroken looking at how corrupt humanity has become.** He wanted to give them blessing and life, but humans chose anger, lust, violence, and evil.

He's given them hundreds of years to turn back to Him. He had Noah build a giant boat in front of all his neighbors. They probably asked him what he was doing, and Noah, being a *"herald of righteousness"* (2 Peter 2:5), probably warned them and invited them back to God. Perhaps he said things like, *"Judgment is coming! But God loves you and has provided a way! Come get on the boat!"*

But even despite this GIGANTIC picture of God's coming judgment *and* the opportunity to be saved, people still refused Him. So God destroys nearly everything in a sort of "un-creation." (Once again, the world is covered in chaotic waters, just like in Genesis 1:2.) But He saves a remnant, a small group of people, all because of one man's faith: Noah.

Now Noah wasn't perfect, of course. God was judging the sin of the world, and in order to be just, that would have to include Noah and his family. But notice what God does. Aside from two of every animal entering the boat, God sets aside seven pairs of clean animals. What will some of these animals be used for? Sacrifices.

Noah offers these animals as a burnt offering to praise God and to cover the sins of him and his family. Once again, we see God Himself providing the sacrifice to rescue His people!

## SCRIPTURE

Matthew 24:35–51

## READ

Jesus references Noah when He's talking about the end of all things. God is going to deal with injustice and evil once and for all. He will destroy everything in a sort of "second flood" (though we know from His promise to Noah that it won't be a literal flood).

Only those who put their faith in this "better Noah," Jesus, will be saved as a remnant. **Where Noah saved his family by paving a way on a wooden boat, we are saved by Christ paving a way on a wooden cross.**

This is great news! After the flood, when Noah left the ark, the world had been sort of "re-created," and God gave Noah similar commands that He had given to Adam and Eve. (And now they can eat meat! Hurray for bacon!) But the world would soon be ruined again by humanity's evil hearts.

In the future, God will save His people from judgment (because Jesus took it for us), and we will go into a world that has been "re-created" even better! *And* our hearts will be fully pure! This whole story foreshadows Jesus rescuing us and calls us to put our faith in Him.

## JOURNAL

**We don't know when the "flood" of Jesus' return is going to occur, but we do know it could be today.** How can this truth affect our relationships? Work? Dreams, goals, and ambitions? How might you stay "ready" like the faithful servant? What needs to change for you to be truly ready, like a servant waiting for his master?

**Noah likely spent anywhere between 55 to 75 years building the ark.** It's true that Christ's return may be 55 to 75 years from now or after you die. What are you "building" in this time? Is it worth it? Is it in response to a call from God? Is it for Him or is it for yourself? If God were to say, *"Build for Me. You decide what,"* what would you build?

## CLOSING PRAYER

*"Jesus, thank You for Noah's example of faithfulness here. May I emulate it in all I do. Thank You for an assured future with You. May I have the confidence and courage to follow through with all You have tasked for me. And may I be faithful to invite others to follow You as well. In Your name, Jesus, amen."*

# 9

# The Tower of Babel

## OPENING PRAYER

*"Father, thank You for being sovereign over my life. You know my history, my parents, and the generations before. Your hand has been upon me. Please bring Your Kingdom deeper into my family that the generations after may glorify You forever. Amen."*

## SCRIPTURE

Genesis 9:18–11:9

## THINK

- *Where is His grace?*
- *Where is His lordship?*
- *What can we learn about the state of humanity?*
- *What themes, ideas, or imagery have we seen before?*

## READ

Despite God's incredible grace, it is clear the sin issue hasn't been solved yet. Noah's story ends with the refrain *"and he died,"* once again reminding us of the generations of spiritual decline in Genesis 5. Noah is not the promised savior, displayed even more clearly when he gets drunk and passes out naked in his tent.

We see Ham dishonoring his father, leading Noah to pronounce a curse on Ham's son, Canaan. Likely, this is more of an acknowledgment that Ham's terrible character will have a detrimental effect on Canaan's character. This prophecy will ring true as the Canaanites will become enemies of God's people later on in the story, along with Ham's other descendants in the Egyptians, Canaanites, and Babylonians (aka Babel).

It's here we get the famous story of the Tower of Babel. Did you catch the themes played out here? God had told Noah and his descendants to be fruitful and multiply and to fill the whole earth, just like He had told Adam and Eve. He wanted His blessing and glory to go and grow everywhere. He always does. It's in His nature!

But these people would rather have glory for themselves, desiring to ascend to God's throne that they may rule like Him. (Remind you of anyone?) They build up Babel, desiring it to be the center of a one-world empire where they are the ones in charge.

Fortunately, God mitigates the evil that this would cause by dividing the people. He causes them to disperse and spread out around the world. And for their own sake! He knows how evil this empire would become if left completely unchecked. He uses the consequences of their evil to accomplish His own original purposes. Later, however, the Holy Spirit is going to flip the script....

After Jesus rises from the dead, His followers meet together in Jerusalem during a holiday Christians now call Pentecost. Jews from all over the world would return to Jerusalem to celebrate. And God does something incredible...

## SCRIPTURE

Acts 2:1–15
Acts 2:22–24
Acts 2:36–41

## READ

God "reverses the curse"! Different languages still exist, but the division between the people is gone. It's almost like the believers belong anywhere in the world just like how humanity was supposed to live. At first, God caused the division to save humanity *from* itself. But now, He brings unity to save humanity *to* Himself.

God doesn't remove the uniqueness of individual cultures like Babel wanted to do. Instead, He enables His beautifully diverse people to worship and glorify Him within their own customs and preferences.

Sometimes being around people from a different culture or background can be intimidating or uncomfortable. But God's heart is for us to rejoice in His creativity. The greater awe we have of God, the greater love and appreciation we can have for people who look and act differently than us.

God wants *all* people to come to know him, regardless of background, race, culture, class, generation, or country. Did you catch how he reached those people in Acts? **He didn't make everyone understand His disciples...He made a way for His disciples to go to them.**

Oftentimes, in order to love and spread the gospel, we need to drop our own preferences and comfort. It can be hard, but amazing things can happen. Here, *three thousand* people put their faith in Jesus that day!

## JOURNAL

**God desires us to love those different than us.** How do you do when you are around people who are different from you? Maybe they dress differently, eat different foods than you, or have a different ethnic background than you. Maybe they do things differently, have different traditions, or value things differently than you. Is it easy or difficult? How? Why is that?

**It was God's idea to have a wide variety of ethnicities and cultures.** Where might you have baseline presumptions about someone based off of their ethnicity or culture? Is there anything in your heart that just doesn't like certain groups of people? Are you harsh on people of your own culture? This can be hard to confess, but be honest with Him. He wants you to see people how *He* sees them.

**We are called to see other believers as brothers and sisters despite the differences in preferences.** Consider some Christians or churches you know that do things differently than you're used to. Are you typically judgmental? Or do you rejoice in how God is being displayed? (Be careful not to confuse preferences with theology!)

**Jesus wants us to lay down our lives for others (Matthew 20:28).** What are some ways you can lay down your preferences in order to love someone or show respect? When can you purposely make yourself less comfortable so others may be more comfortable?

## CLOSING PRAYER

*"Lord, You are greater than me. And it is better for me to lay down my preferences if it means loving someone better and sharing the gospel with them. Please help me have a humble heart when encountering people who are different from me. Amen."*

# THE PATRIARCH ERA

# PART II: THE PATRIARCH ERA

## SUMMARY

*God initiates a special relationship with a dysfunctional family, promising to use them in a key role in His plan to redeem the world.*

## THE SCRIPTURE OF THIS ERA

Genesis 12–50
Job

## INTRODUCTION

Our transition between the Creation and Patriarch eras is marked by another genealogy. In Genesis 11:10–32, it appears the effects of sin and being deprived of eating from the Tree of Life has taken its toll on the human body's ability to live for hundreds of years. Yet here, there is no mention of the *"and he died"* phrase we had back in Genesis 5. So what's going on?

Despite the decline of humanity, God is tracing the path of life from Shem to Abram. Ultimately, it's going to be the path of that promised offspring of Eve through Abraham's family to Christ.

The Patriarch Era brings us into the next phase of God's plan to redeem the world, and it centers around four fathers and their highly dysfunctional families. Often these families will do incredibly terrible things, and we are often left wondering what God is doing and why He chose to work with these people.

At the very end of the era in Genesis 50:20, we read this: ***"As for you, you meant evil against me, but God meant it for good, to bring it about that many people should be kept alive, as they are today."*** We will learn the exact context of this verse, but it can certainly be used to help us understand how God is going to work throughout this era. Namely, He will orchestrate events through the actions of people to accomplish His good will to save lives.

This era focuses on the stories of Abraham, Isaac, Jacob, and Joseph, beginning with God's call to Abraham and ending with Jacob's family in Egypt under Joseph's protection. It is also believed that the story of Job takes place during this era. His story doesn't interact with the main Patriarch storyline, so we won't be covering it in this study.

# 10

# The Call of Abram

## OPENING PRAYER

*"God, You are so great. Thank You for calling me to follow You and inviting me into a friendship with You. You are so kind to me. May I hear Your voice today. Amen!"*

## SCRIPTURE

Genesis 11:27–12:9

## THINK

- *Where is His grace?*
- *Where is His lordship?*
- *What might be some unique struggles Abram would have had being called at 75 years old to follow God?*

## READ

Here we meet our next major player in God's plan to redeem the world: Abram, who will later be renamed Abraham. He's a seemingly random old man with a barren wife from Chaldea, which is a city in ancient Babylon. (We'll refer to it as Babylon to keep this theme in front of us.) This is the man God calls out of nowhere.

To obey God, Abram must *go from* a few things. First, his country: Babylon. We will find out later that Abram is going to leave this nation so God can establish a new nation out of him.

But there's also a spiritual element here. Abram grew up in the heart of the wicked culture that attempted to build that "tower to the heavens" all those years ago. And now God is calling him out of it, in an act of *separating* to accomplish His purposes. He sets Abram aside for a special purpose, calling him to abandon the way Babylon sees the world.

God then specifies that Abram must leave his kindred. This means his culture, his preferences, his friends that don't follow God...what a challenge! But God's plan is to make him into a new people, a new culture.

But then God takes it a step further (which He often does). He tells Abram to leave *"his father's house."* Now on one hand, God had already been quietly leading Abram slowly out of Babylon (Gen. 11:31), but it's after his father dies that God speaks.

The voice of Abram's father must have no more influence over him. God calls Abram to break from the sinful holds of the prior generations. Not only will God Himself be a father to Abram, but He will also make Abram into a new sort of father.

When God calls us, there's usually a pattern. He calls us *from* something and *to* another. And in the middle is the choice of our obedience. If Abram wants to obey, he needs to pack up and follow God to...

...wait, where?

*"...to the land that I will show you."*

What kind of answer is that?!

It's the one God considers good to give him. So Abram is faced with a choice: Follow his nation, his kindred, and his father's path? Or let God make him into a new nation, a new kindred, and a new father? Abram can't have it both ways.

## SCRIPTURE

Hebrews 11:8–10
John 14:1–3

## READ

Hebrews 11 tells us that Abram (aka Abraham) obeyed God, looking to **where he was going** and not focused on **what he was leaving**. Hebrews clarifies that it wasn't just the promises listed in Genesis 12; God revealed to him a future city that He Himself would establish.

Even though he didn't know what God's promises would fully look like (or even *where* the land was!), **he trusted God's character and authority**. Jesus invites us to do the same. Right now, He is in Heaven preparing a place for us—that same future city Abram was looking forward to.

Sometimes obeying God can be tough because of what we hold on to or value. We become very focused on the *"from's"* instead of the *"to's."*

The night before He was crucified, Jesus told His disciples not to be afraid of losing Him but to focus on where He was going *to*. This would give them hope and power to be obedient and trust God in all their daily decisions. *Going* will be tough at times, but it's easier when *"to"* is more important to you than *"from."*

Jesus left *from* heaven and *obeyed* by going *to* the cross. Jesus knows what it's like to leave what's comfortable to do what's hard or seemingly impossible! Then after He rose from the dead, He left *from* earth and *obeyed* by going back *to* heaven. Jesus knows it can be hard to obey, **so He invites us to be like Him and focus on where we are going *to*!**

## JOURNAL

**Abram had to leave his country, his kindred (people and culture), and his household (parents' leadership).** Is God asking you to leave your country? Aspects of your "people" and culture? Aspects of your parents' influence? What might be some other things God is calling you "from"? "To"?

**Abram was able to be faithful because he kept his heart set on God's Kingdom.** How do you tend to respond to God's calls on your life? Is it out of anticipation for His Kingdom? Guilt to do better? Embarrassment from how long you've been a Christian? Obligation? Begrudgingly? How would focusing your heart on God's Kingdom change the way you respond in faith?

## CLOSING PRAYER

*"Jesus, it's easy for me to be distracted and caught up in the things right in front of me and what I'm comfortable with. Please help me focus on what You want for me over what I want. Thank You for helping me practice obedience to You, my Friend. I love You so much! Amen."*

# 11

# Down to Egypt

## OPENING PRAYER

*"Father, I really appreciate You helping me make space for this time together. Would you please help me focus my attention on You now. YOU are the reason I am here. YOU are here with me now. YOU are the God of the universe. YOU are my joy. I love YOU, my Lord."*

## SCRIPTURE

Genesis 12:10–20

## THINK

- *Where is His grace?*
- *Where is His lordship?*
- *What motivates Abram's actions in this story? What motivates God's?*

## READ

After a great showing of faith from Abram in our last passage, we see a major failure here. This is going to be a pattern we will sadly see often in this family.

First, in a desperate time of need, Abram goes to Egypt for aid rather than God. Keep this move in the back of your mind because this will happen over and over again in Scripture.

Abram then considers his own life more valuable than his wife's. Sarai (who is later renamed Sarah) is supposed to be his best friend and the woman God is going to use to bring about His promises...and yet Abram chooses fear, self-preservation, and distrust.

Abram then acts like Satan as he *deceives* Pharaoh. Pharaoh is actually shocked someone would do something like this. It's a profoundly ironic moment where a man who proclaims to be a god is disturbed by the actions of a man who is supposed to be a follower of the true God.

But God is incredibly gracious here. He sends plagues on an entire country to keep Sarai from being harmed, so He can keep His promises from being broken and to carry out His plan for our salvation.

Revelation 21 shows us that Jesus' bride is the church. Fortunately, we have a God who put His bride before Himself. Look at what Jesus did for His bride when He stood before authorities endangering His life...

## SCRIPTURE

Luke 22:66–71

## READ

Jesus didn't disown His bride like Abram did. He *owned* His relationship with her! **Where Abram received lots of material goods from the ruler of Egypt at the expense of his bride, Jesus received beatings and a crucifixion for His bride.**

Abram could have chosen trust in God's promises and chosen his wife over himself in this circumstance, but he didn't. He didn't **own his relationship** with God or his wife when the going got tough. **Jesus calls us to really own our relationship with Him.** The stakes are incredibly high. Look at this warning from Jesus...

## SCRIPTURE

Luke 12:8–9

## READ

Now this doesn't mean you need to walk around wearing a shirt that says *"I love Jesus"* everywhere you go. What it *does* mean is that when faced with pressure, we **own our relationship with Jesus**. We obey Him when others tell us not to. We share that our faith in Jesus is what motivates us to do certain things. If told to *"deny Jesus or die,"* we choose death.

Though that may be unlikely in your current context, Christians all over the world throughout history (and even today) are faced with that choice. We should have it already set in our minds to choose death.

**Like Jesus, we are called to own our relationship with God in every circumstance and in every aspect of our lives, both in good times and bad.** So the question is: Do you?

## JOURNAL

**When you really own something, it means you live it.** If you really own being a Buffalo Bills fan, you watch all their games, buy all their merch, know all the stats of the players...it is part of who you are. What would it mean for you to really own your relationship with Jesus?

**Big decisions of faithfulness are easier to make when hundreds of little decisions of faithfulness have been made.** Though you may not have any big decisions to make right now, what are little decisions of faithfulness (owning your relationship with Jesus) you can make now? (Examples: praying for your family, being positive towards a classmate or coworker, being hard-working in all you do, etc.)

**Saying "yes to Jesus" now will prepare you to be faithful in future circumstances.** What are some possible future events you can predetermine to say "yes to Jesus" to now? Losing a job? Losing a loved one? War breaking out? An argument with a friend? Ask God to help you set faithfulness in your heart and mind now!

**Abram folded under the pressures of a difficult circumstance (a famine) and an intimidating authority (Pharaoh).** Are there any areas right now you fold to? Circumstances that seem out of God's control? People who are bigger than God in your eyes? Take time confessing these things to God and ask Him to give you the courage to stay faithful in light of them.

### CLOSING PRAYER

*"Jesus, it can be easy for me to choose comfort and ease rather than faithfulness to You. It can be easy for me to choose fear over trust in You. Please help me see clearly and choose faithfulness in all things today. Thank You for helping me practice obedience to You. I love You, Lord. Amen."*

# 12

# Counted as Righteousness

## OPENING PRAYER

*"Dear God, You are so good to me. Thank You for the faith You have given me. Thank You for joy in You. Thank You for peace in You. Please open my ears to hear You during this time. Amen!"*

## SCRIPTURE

Genesis 15

## THINK

- *Where is His grace?*
- *Where is His lordship?*
- *How would you answer if someone were to ask you, "How do I get to Heaven?"*

## READ

This passage has a huge implication to our faith, and it has to do with this idea of **righteousness**. To be righteous means to be in "right standing." **To be in "right standing" with the law means you are not**

**guilty of any crimes. You have a clean record and no judgment from the courts coming your way.**

Because of sin, **by default we are unrighteous** before God. We are naturally rebellious. It means we have broken God's law and are not in "right standing." We are guilty of our crimes, so something needs to be done, just like when laws are broken in society. We call this **justice.**

So how does one become righteous again? How do we have "right standing" before God and His law? Let's look at our story of Abram…

Between this chapter and chapter 12, God gives Abram three promises:

1. He will build a nation out of Abram.
2. He will give that nation land.
3. He will bless the world through that nation.

This agreement is often referred to as the **Abrahamic Covenant.** But Abram has some doubts. Sarai is well past child-bearing years, and he wonders how this is going to happen.

So God seals His promises through the ceremony seen here, including a prophecy about his family being slaves for 400 years…

But look at verse 6 again. Abram **believed** God at His word, and God essentially says "Okay, Abram is in 'right standing' with Me and My law."

So is belief all it takes to be good with God??

## SCRIPTURE

Romans 4:16–25

## READ

We see here that God will count us as being in "right standing" if we *"believe in Him who raised from the dead Jesus our Lord."* To "believe" is not simply to acknowledge something as true, but to accept a truth in such a way that causes you to live differently. This may sound confusing, but picture it this way…

You are on trial before God. You've sinned, which means you've committed a crime against God's government. So there must be a penalty for your actions.

God is sitting in the judge's chair, and the verdict is that you are going to be kicked out of God's kingdom and sent to Hell. It's like how a criminal must get kicked out of society and sent to prison for his actions.

You say to God, *"God, I promise if You put me in 'right standing' before the law, I won't break it again!"* But really? You know that's not true. How could you possibly remain perfect the rest of your life?

So you say, *"God, I know You love me. Can't You just let me go free?"* But God reminds you He loves everyone. Is He supposed to let everyone off as well and just let them continue doing evil? What about the victims of their crimes? Would they call God a just judge?

So you say, *"Well, God, can't You just make everyone automatically perfect?"* But God reminds you that not everyone *wants* to follow God. They don't like His definition of good and evil. Should He just force them? No, He wants them to have the choice to follow Him out of love for Him. He wants a genuine relationship with us.

You say, *"But God, I'm not as evil as they are. How about You let the people who are trying to be good go free?"* But God reminds you that He can't play favorites with people. That wouldn't be a just thing to do. Just like in society, it doesn't matter if a driver meant to be speeding or was speeding on purpose; they must pay a fine if they were speeding.

But then God the Judge says this, *"I'll tell you what. My son, Jesus, has never broken the law. I'm making an offer that He will pay that fine for you. You get His record and He gets yours. If you agree, then you will be in 'right standing' before me. What do you say?"*

You say, *"But God, you know I'm going to break the law again. I hate it, but I can't help it."* He says, *"I know. My Son is covering for those also. Part of this agreement means you leave here with the Holy Spirit who will help you live in my Kingdom from now on. So do we have a deal?"*

To believe would be to accept that offer from God, living differently because of the incredible mercy He's shown you.

## JOURNAL

**Take some time to sit quietly and really put yourself in this scenario.** If you agreed, how would you leave that courtroom? How would that change you? Take some time to thank Jesus for making a way to have "right standing" with Him.

**Abram believed God before expressing his doubts.** This order is important. Why? What benefits are there to expressing doubts after belief?

**God uses the stars as a picture of His promise to Abram.** Why do you think He decided to do that? Why are pictures important? What other pictures in Scripture can you recall? Are there any pictures He has given you personally for you to remember?

## CLOSING PRAYER

*"My good Judge, thank You for Your offer. Thank You for the free gift of grace. Thank You for finding a way to be both just and merciful. May I be just and merciful in all I do. Thank You. Thank You. Thank You. Amen."*

# 13

# Hagar & Ishmael

## OPENING PRAYER

*"Dear Lord, thank You for this time together. Thank You for the good things You are doing this week, even when it's difficult to notice them. Would You please bring life out of this time together with You? Amen."*

## SCRIPTURE

Genesis 16

## THINK

- *Where is His grace?*
- *Where is His lordship?*

## READ

Can we say major disaster? Yes. Let's list a few... First, Sarai blames God for not letting her get pregnant. And while it's true in one way, God is doing this so everyone will know that this is a miracle. But Sarai's attitude is accusatory instead of trusting. God cares a lot about our attitude.

Then Sarai tells her husband to have an affair with Hagar, and Abram foolishly agrees. (The reality of the power disparity between Abram and one of his slaves makes this even all the more evil.) Perhaps you made the connection that Hagar is an Egyptian slave. When did she join them? Most likely after Pharaoh kicked them out of Egypt! So we have that coming back to haunt them.

Look at the similarities here with Adam and Eve. Eve **TOOK** the fruit and gave it to her husband to eat, and Sarai **TOOK** Hagar and gave her to her husband to sleep with. Same old story.

Then after Hagar gets pregnant, Sarai gets incredibly jealous and starts mistreating her so badly that Hagar runs away. Abram, meanwhile, is completely passive and stays out of it. Later, we're going to read about how God wants us to take care of foreigners and immigrants, and this is literally the exact opposite of doing that.

Fortunately, God's heart towards the immigrant is still gracious. He saves Hagar, tells her to go back (where she will ultimately be safer than out in the desert), and promises to make a great nation out of Ishmael.

Over time, Ishmael's descendants will establish the Islamic religion. Today, there are still wars between the descendants of Isaac (Judaism) and Ishmael (Islam) in the Middle East, all because of Abram and Sarai's actions. It's incredibly tragic.

Sadly, we can be pretty similar to Sarai and Abram. When things don't go our way, we tend to react and do stupid things. Praise God that Jesus stayed faithful despite His agony over the Father's plan. Take a look at this story the night before Jesus' crucifixion...

## SCRIPTURE

Luke 22:39–44

## READ

Jesus preferred His mission to save us to go another way. He was honest with the Father about it. He asked for another option. But at the end of the day, He said yes to the Father's plan, even if it made His life more difficult. We are called to do the same.

**Abram and Sarai did the *easier* thing instead of the *godly* thing, which made things *disastrous*. But Jesus did the *harder* thing, the *godly* thing, which made things *glorious*.** It's because of Jesus' faithfulness that we are able to experience all the glories of God.

There are things in our lives that we wish were different. Life is promised to be filled with hardships, difficult choices, terrible circumstances, and trials of various kinds. Maybe, like Sarai, you are in a tough season of waiting.

So the choice we have is to either be like Abram and Sarai or to be like Jesus. **Both will have consequences. We get to choose whether they're disastrous or ultimately glorious.**

## JOURNAL

**Sarai's impatience and frustration was rooted in distrust of God's promises, which is a distrust in God.** What are you currently frustrated by? Impatient with? Can you identify how these things may be rooted in a distrust towards God?

**Sarai doesn't take her impatience and frustration to God.** Instead, she takes it to her husband and ultimately into her own hands.

When was a time you took things "out of God's hands" and placed them in another's hands? In your own hands? How might things have turned out differently if you hadn't? Is there anything now you need to take out of your own hands and return to God?

**Abram sins greatly by passivity.** He listens to Sarai's request to sin as Adam listened to Eve's back in the garden. He lets Sarai abuse Hagar and send her out into the desert. Is there any sin in your life you are allowing via passivity? Is there anyone you have influence or authority over you are allowing to sin via passivity? (Think children, employees, maybe even needing to gently correct your spouse...)

**Abram and Sarai's sin led to conflicts that are still happening today.** Can you identify any sins of past generations that have affected your life directly or indirectly? What are some ways God has halted, prevented, or turned around sins that came from those before you? Is there anything in your life now that very well may cause disaster in the generations after you?

## CLOSING PRAYER

*"Father, my life is going to be very hard at times. May I be a child of Yours that chooses godliness over easiness every time. May I have a deep and abiding trust in You. Thank You for being with me as I grow. I love You so much! Amen."*

# 14

# Sarah Laughs

## OPENING PRAYER

*"God, You are a crazy God sometimes. You always do the unexpected, and I love that about You. Would You give me eyes to see You at work even when it seems crazy to me? May my hope be in who You are and not the circumstances around me. Amen."*

## SCRIPTURE

Genesis 17:15–21
Genesis 18:1–15

## THINK

- *Where is His grace?*
- *Where is His lordship?*
- *Look up the meanings of the names Abram, Abraham, Sarai, Sarah, and Isaac. (Your Bible may have footnotes on them.) What is significant about these name changes? What do you think that did to Abraham's and Sarah's mindset? Why do you think God did this?*

## READ

Despite Abraham's failure with Hagar, God once again reconfirms the covenant He made with him. Abraham's own unfaithfulness will not thwart God's plans.

This is a beautiful story of hilarious awkwardness. The newly renamed Abraham and Sarah are told again that Sarah will give birth in her old age. Both laugh at the idea, but Sarah's the one who lies when asked about it. And then she's called out immediately for lying.

Genesis 18:15 is perhaps the most awkward moment in the entire Bible. You can't help but squirm at the feeling of discomfort.

What God is saying is so utterly ridiculous to her. But God is a fan of doing the miraculous and the ridiculous. Check out this story of Jesus...

## SCRIPTURE

Matthew 17:24–27

## READ

RIGHT?!? Jesus just casually teaches a lesson by telling Peter to get a coin out of a fish's mouth to pay His taxes. (Yes, even Jesus paid taxes. It's impossible to escape...)

Now in both instances, God is doing something wild to teach us. With Abraham and Sarah, the one thing God wants us to know is that it is *He* who will fulfill His promises. It won't be an accident or coincidence.

In the fish story, Jesus is using the tax as a metaphor of how our relationship with God will change from *"others"* to *"children"* through His sacrifice.

But what I want us to see is God's habit of using the miraculous and the ridiculous to accomplish His will. Keep an eye out for it as we go through the Bible. It's everywhere!

Something important for us to know about the "ridiculous calls" of God is that God wants us to give *Him* the glory. From giant miracles to small day-to-day provision, our hearts should be praising *Him* first.

But there's something to be careful of here. There may be times when you *think* you are hearing from God, and it sounds ridiculous. But just because it *sounds* ridiculous doesn't necessarily mean it's from God.

We live in a story-oriented world, and it's natural to see ourselves as the main character of that story. So sometimes we imagine ourselves in the middle of a story with a ridiculous opportunity and think, *"It's so wild, it just has to be from God! I'm the main character, and this is my opportunity to seize it, and God is going to bless it!"* (Did you notice **SEEING** the opportunity, **CONSIDERING IT GOOD**, and then **TAKING** it?)

Perhaps it's a once-in-a-lifetime job opportunity: *"I've got to take it!"*

Perhaps someone you've been attracted to is finally single: *"This is the sign they belong with me!"*

Perhaps you received a bonus out of nowhere: *"God must want me to buy that new car I've been wanting!"*

Even though God does the ridiculous, it doesn't mean that the ridiculous is necessarily from God. So here are three recommendations of things to do when you think you are hearing something ridiculous from God:

**1) Tell someone you trust and who loves Jesus about it.** And then *listen* to their feedback. God calls us to live in community and obey together. Humility is crucial to discerning God's voice. (Abraham wasn't alone in his call. He was partners with Sarah!)

**2) Ask yourself, *"Will doing this ridiculous thing lead to God's glory or mine?"*** If it leads to yours alone, it probably isn't from God. He's not about that. (Abraham's calling was ultimately to bring blessing to the world for Jesus, remember?) Don't get me wrong, success can be a great and godly thing. But your success should always point to how awesome God is.

**3) Is this thing I'm hearing *consistent* from what I know about God's *character* in the Bible?** An extreme example would be, *"I think God would approve of me cheating on my spouse because He wants me to be happy."* Yeeahh…no. More often than not, it will be subtle. It's important for us to really know God and our Bible well so we're not deceived by the enemy or our own passing desires!

## JOURNAL

**The work God promised to do through Abraham and Sarah sounded ridiculous.** Have you ever experienced a ridiculous call that was from God? A ridiculous call you realized wasn't from God? Is there anything now you believe is from God that you should probably rethink, going through the prompts listed above?

**Abraham's faith required humility.** Do you have the humility to truly receive input from others about the dreams you may have? About your opportunities or goals? Are you willing to really have those things you consider from God come under scrutiny? Perhaps it's a job opportunity, an ambition, or a relationship you desire.

**It's easy for us to think that God affirms the things we approve of.** If you were really honest with yourself, do you have a habit of focusing on what brings you glory over what brings God glory? Do you look to the Bible to make sure that what you hear is consistent with God's character? Or do you instead try to find Bible passages that make your ideas sound good?

## CLOSING PRAYER

*"God, I would really like to see You do some ridiculous things in my life and in the lives of those around me. Would You give me eyes to see them? Please create in me a humble heart to hear Your call and the courage to be obedient. I love You, Lord. Amen."*

# 15

# Abraham Lies...Again...

## OPENING PRAYER

*"Lord God, You are awesome! You are wonderful! You are glorious! You are great! You are kind! You are fun! You are adventurous! You are worthy of all my praise! Thank You for being my Good Teacher. I love You."*

## SCRIPTURE

Genesis 20

## THINK

- *Where is His grace?*
- *Where is His lordship?*
- *How could Abraham have done the same sinful action again?*
- *How was Abraham justifying his actions?*

## READ

How in the world could Abraham do the same thing again?! Didn't he know better? Didn't he learn his lesson? Didn't he hear from God??

**If you're beating up on Abraham right now, it may be because you think you're better than everyone else or because you're really hard on yourself.**

The reality is that we all sin. And there will be times when you will be surprised by your own sinfulness. You'll look at yourself and think, *"I didn't know I was capable of doing that!"* If it hasn't happened yet, it will. It's not an excuse but rather a sad reality of being sinful by default.

But look at God's faithfulness and mercy on literally everyone. First, He is committed to fulfilling His promises. He's going to use Abraham and Sarah to bring about the promise whether they are faithful or not. He protects Sarah from her husband's foolishness again *and* keeps Abraham from being killed by Abimelech.

Remember how God said He would bless those who bless Abraham and curse those who curse him? Well Abimelech happens to bless Abraham with loads of material goods, and so God blesses Abimelech by healing him and opening the wombs of his people's women. (God says over and over again in the Bible that children are a blessing, so to keep women from having children would be keeping them from experiencing that blessing!)

## SCRIPTURE

2 Timothy 2:11–13
1 John 1:9

## READ

When God commits to something, He commits regardless of our faithfulness. **God will always be God even when we are not the people we are supposed to be.** This is good news! It is a reminder that we are forgiven through Jesus for *all* of our sins, including the ones we haven't done yet.

Now you may ask, *"If God is going to forgive me, can't I just do whatever I want?"*

Jesus endured the wrath of God for your sake. Sit with that idea for a while...would you really *want* to sin against someone who already has taken the punishment for our sins, especially when we don't deserve it?

It'd be a really awful attitude to have with someone who is trying to bring you joy, peace, laughter, adventure...If that's your attitude, do you really *want* God to be King of your life? Or do you want to be like Adam and Eve and be your own king instead?

It's your call. There's only one throne. It can't be both of you.

God desires for us to have healthy attitudes towards sin. Sin is serious. Jesus sacrificed Himself because of it. *And alongside that,* the righteousness ("right standing") we have because of Jesus and the Holy Spirit living inside us helps us move forward.

After he sinned, was Abraham so discouraged in himself that he just gave up following God? Did he just think, *"God, I'm a terrible person. I shouldn't even be loved by You. Pick someone else for Your plan!"* No! Abraham, despite his sin, needed to keep going, and so do you. And here's how...

**1) CONFESS:** Confession is agreeing with God that you've sinned. Say it out loud to Him or with someone. Acknowledge it. Ask for forgiveness—not to get your salvation again (that never changes) but to restore your relationship with Him. In confessing what we have been doing/thinking/feeling wrong, we experience His active forgiveness in our day-to-day lives.

**2) REPENT:** It literally means "turn around." So turn around *from* the direction you were going (sinful behavior/thinking) and fix your eyes to Jesus, your King.

**3) MOVE ON:** It means keep learning, loving, and walking with Jesus. Don't beat yourself up. Don't listen to Satan's accusations. Don't believe you are guilty. You are in "right standing" before God! Just let it go and do what you need to do to follow Jesus at this moment. Wallowing in guilt prevents us from experiencing freedom and the blessings that come from knowing we are forgiven. And He's got work He wants to do through you!

## JOURNAL

**We all have "patterns of sinfulness."** In other words, we typically have 3–5 ways we sin consistently. It's not an excuse, but it can be a reality for a time. Maybe you struggle with anger, lying, or greed. Maybe you tend to be arrogant or (the opposite) demean yourself. What are 3–5 ways you tend to sin regularly? Then spend some time confessing (agreeing with Jesus about your sin), repenting (fixing your eyes on Jesus), and moving on (away *from* your way *towards* God's way).

**God knew Abimelech was innocent and stepped in to keep him from sinning.** (And notice how Abimelech obeyed immediately when he *"rose early in the morning"*?) Have you ever experienced God doing this in your life? Ask God now for clarity to see anything you may be stepping into by accident. He doesn't want you to sin!

**Abraham used a truth about Sarah being his half-sister to justify sinful actions.** When was a time you've done something wrong justifying it with facts? Are you doing it now in any areas of your life?

## CLOSING PRAYER

*"God, You are always faithful. May I be faithful like You. My heart and mind naturally want to sin. Would you change that so I would hate the idea of sinning against You? And would You help me not beat myself up when I sin, but trust in Your faithfulness? Thank You for loving me. I love You too. Amen."*

# 16

# Abraham Sacrifices Isaac

## OPENING PRAYER

*"Dear God, thank You for this time together. Thank You for wanting a deeper relationship with me. You are always trying to get my attention. You are always trying to share Your love and grace with me. May I receive Your love and grace during this time together. In Jesus' name, amen."*

## SCRIPTURE

Genesis 21:1–7
Genesis 22:1–19
Hebrews 11:17–19

## THINK

• *Where is His grace?*
• *Where is His lordship?*
• *How do you think someone grows in faith?*

## READ

God has finally provided that miracle child for Abraham and Sarah. He has been faithful to fulfill His promises! And they are praising God for the joy He has given them in this baby boy. All of their dreams for a family have finally come true.

And then God asks Abraham to do the impossible.

This test from God can be really hard to swallow, but if you take time to sit with it, it could be a game-changer in your relationship with God. And the biggest takeaway is *not* looking at Abraham's faith, but looking at *God's faithfulness* so that our faith grows. Abraham obviously shows a great amount of faith here, but it's because of one thing: **He trusts God's *character*.**

We see from Genesis 22:1 that God is testing Abraham. There could be a variety of reasons for the trials we face. It could be a consequence of our sin or that we were sinned against or just a reality of living in a sinful world...but there will be times when God brings us trials to test our faith.

We won't always know if it is a test or even why God is testing us, but we can trust that God always acts for good.

So regardless of the kind of trial, our responsibility is to choose faith. To choose obedience. Look at how quickly Abraham obeys God (Genesis 22:3).

Our Hebrews passage gives us a hint as to why Abraham was so "easily" able to obey God: **He *"received the promises"* of God.** In other words, He knew God is faithful to keep His promises. He had made a promise to bring blessing through Isaac. God doesn't break His promises. So Abraham must've thought God would either stop him at the last minute or raise Isaac from the dead.

See it's not our performance that increases our faith. It's not bettering ourselves or doing the right thing even. It's not even reading our Bibles and praying regularly. **Our faith grows when our understanding of *who God is* grows.** (We do this *through* reading the Bible and praying, of course!)

It's hard to trust someone you don't know. Why would you? But the more you get to know God with the help of the Holy Spirit, the more you will naturally trust Him. This is *way* better than trying to just "be a better Christian."

Knowing *who* God is will increase our faith. So read your Bible and pray regularly, but not to be "a good Christian who does the right things," but instead to really get to know God!

## SCRIPTURE

Romans 8:31–39

## READ

This passage in Romans encourages us to be courageous. Why? Because of God's character. See, **where Abraham's son was spared, God's Son was not.** God followed through and sacrificed His own Son, Jesus. In a way, God passed His own test. That's how faithful God is.

So because of *His* faithfulness, we can have confidence that we are not condemned (aka we are in "right standing") in verse 34...

That nothing can separate us from His love for us (verses 35 and 38-39)...

That we are *"more than conquerors"* over our sin, the devil, and the world (verse 37).

Praise God!

## JOURNAL

**It's knowing God and His character that fuels our faith.** Write out some aspects of God's character that have been encouraging to you lately. Or think of some right now that are encouraging to you. Praise Him for these things!

**Think over some areas in your life where it may be hard to trust God.** How might some of the things you just listed in the previous question strengthen your faith? Embolden you? Encourage you?

**Like with Noah before and Jesus after, God is the one who provided the sacrifice.** When were some times when God stepped in on your behalf? When has He provided blessing out of nowhere? How did you respond to that time? Is there a way He would like you to live differently now as you remember those things?

## CLOSING PRAYER

*"Jesus, I want to have faith like Abraham. I want to know You better as my Friend. I want to trust You more naturally. Would You open my eyes and heart to really see You and know You? I love You, my Lord and Friend. Amen."*

# 17

# The Call of Rebekah

## OPENING PRAYER

*"Hello, Friend. Thank You for being so good to me and for using this study to help me grow in my friendship with You. I'd really like for it to grow some more today. Would You please help me focus and enjoy Your presence? Amen!"*

## READ

In Genesis 23, Sarah dies and Abraham buys a place to bury her. It's the first bit of property Abraham has owned this entire time and a slow beginning of God fulfilling His promise to give him land. It's a beautiful fulfillment in a tragic time.

God will even use sorrow to accomplish His good. But now it's time to move to the next generation.

Now remember, Abraham is living as a wanderer in the land of the Canaanites. So he doesn't want Isaac to risk leaving the land, but he doesn't want him to marry a Canaanite either. They aren't exactly the most godly people.

He wants his son to marry someone who will push him closer to God and fulfill the promise for a nation. (See how important marriage is to God?)

Well, if you're unmarried and the Lord puts it on your heart someday to pursue marriage, pray that the Lord will lead you to someone who follows God's leading like Abraham's servant and Rebekah...

## SCRIPTURE

Genesis 24

## THINK

- *Where is His grace?*
- *Where is His lordship?*
- *How would you describe the servant's character?*
- *How would you describe Rebekah's character?*

## READ

The servant's journey was about 550 miles and would have taken about 21 days to travel by camel. Abraham thought so highly of this servant's character that he entrusted him with helping to fulfill God's promise for building a nation through Isaac and his wife-to-be. The servant makes the trek but realizes what he is doing will have huge consequences. This was an incredibly important mission! So what does he do?

**He seeks God's leading.** He knows God has to be the one to provide. And he *wants* God to be the one to provide a wife for Isaac. He asks God to "be Himself" by asking Him to show *"steadfast love"* to Abraham, which the Bible says over and over again is a huge characteristic of God. The servant has seen God work in Abraham's life and **is now depending on *His* character** to bring Isaac a wife.

And God is faithful! God answers the servant's prayer exactly! (*Mini-lesson: We should never be afraid to ask God for specifics in our prayers. He is a good God!*) We meet Rebekah, who has incredible character. She is hard-working, generous, and hospitable. These are all aspects of God's character too! But this is nothing next to how this story ends.

After learning about the servant's prayer and God's answer, Rebekah knows that God is calling her to be Isaac's wife. But her family doesn't quite want her to leave just yet (and some may be more interested in Abraham's wealth...). So look at God's call to her....

She needs to go **FROM** her country, her people, and her family **TO** a land she has never visited **TO** marry a man she has never met **TO** be a part of God's plan to bless the world. Sounds a bit familiar, right? It's just like God's call to Abraham! And just like Abraham, she **GOES**!

The servant and Rebekah are both *willing* to go when God directs them. They know God's leading in the unknown is the most important. And beyond seeking God's leading and being willing, they both *go*.

Today, the Holy Spirit is the one who leads those in Christ. Check out this story of Him leading Paul...

## SCRIPTURE

Acts 20:22–24

## READ

In context, God is fulfilling His promise to bless the world by having Paul tell people about Jesus, and now He wants Paul to go to Jerusalem. And Paul is going to suffer there as part of His plan.

Now did Paul know every detail of the suffering? No. Did God give the servant Rebekah's name or appearance? Or even assurance that his mission would be successful? No. Did God tell Rebekah about Isaac's personality, income, or career? No.

See, God doesn't share every aspect of His plans with us. He's got so many things going on, we wouldn't even be able to follow it once He started to explain. But He *has* shared with us His big-picture plan to save people through Jesus. The rest of the details aren't as important for us to know all at once.

God doesn't desire us to be robots or "perfect little Christians who always do the right thing." He wants us to have a deep enough friendship with Him so that we simply trust Him in the mystery.

## JOURNAL

**Think about the past several days.** How aware have you been of the Holy Spirit's leading? How intentional have you been in seeking the Holy Spirit? Write down how you would like to see yourself grow in this area.

**Abraham's servant was prayerful on behalf of Abraham and Isaac.** Who can you be prayerful for? Whose good can you be intentionally seeking? How might you love someone this week by going out of your way to bless them?

**Rebekah displayed remarkable character in this story.** How do you respond when someone asks you to serve them? Do you go above and beyond like Rebekah did, expecting nothing in return? Would others describe you as hard-working, generous, and thoughtful? Do you put yourself in a position to serve others?

## CLOSING PRAYER

*"Dear God, thank You for giving me the Holy Spirit. May I become more aware of His leading and more faithful in the moment. May I have a supernatural desire to obey You in all things. I love You, Lord. Amen."*

# 18

# Esau's "Raw" Moment

## OPENING PRAYER

*"Father, there are a lot of things trying to get my attention away from You. Not all of them are bad things, and some of them I do need to focus on...but would you please help me focus on You during this time? This is what's most important right now. Thank You, Lord. I love You."*

## THINK

*How would you describe yourself when you are really hungry? Really angry? Sad? Tired? How are you at making good decisions during those times?*

## SCRIPTURE

Genesis 25:19–34

## THINK

- *Where is His grace?*
- *Where is His lordship?*
- *What was motivating Esau's actions? Jacob's?*

## READ

Before this passage, Abraham died of old age (Genesis 25:8). And here we are introduced to the next generation. The promises of the Abrahamic Covenant (build a nation, give them land, bless the world through them) have been passed on to Isaac and presumably will go to the firstborn, Esau. But God gives Rebekah a hint that things might not go as planned...

Could you relate to Esau here at all? Let's be honest. We can all be a bit dramatic at times. Typically, when we are really "raw" emotionally (hungry, angry, sad, lonely, stressed, or tired), we are more prone to making stupid decisions. We say things or do things we regret. Even in the moment, we justify our behavior only to admit later we acted foolishly. (That is, unless you are too foolish to admit you acted foolishly...)

Jacob's name means "deceiver," and he lives up to it. He takes advantage of his foolish brother in a moment of raw vulnerability.

Maybe you've experienced this. A sibling knows you're in a bad mood, so they mess with you to make things worse. (Or maybe *you* have been that sibling.) But when someone takes advantage of your emotional vulnerability, does that mean you are innocent of all your actions? Of course not!

Verse 34 tells us that Esau *"despised"* his birthright. **His emotional outburst actually *revealed* a shortcoming in his character.** Esau didn't value his future (though he would later when he loses even more).

Now, yes, Jacob is obviously guilty of evil here, but we'll spend more time with him later. For now, it's important for us to know that our raw moments actually *reveal* our true character.

## SCRIPTURE

Matthew 4:1–4

## READ

Jesus experienced those raw moments too. He got hungry, angry, sad, lonely, and tired just like us. But His character was revealed when the deceiver came. Despite being hungry (and probably tired too), Jesus *chose* to trust God's word. He *chose* to not be deceived. He *chose* not to give in to the temptation to **TAKE** the food the devil was offering Him. These raw moments reveal to us that **at His core, Jesus loved honoring His Father more than anything.**

When we sin in those raw moments, we have a tendency to blame it on something else. But anger doesn't excuse our actions. Sadness doesn't excuse our actions. Stress, loneliness, fear, hunger...none of those are excuses for disobedience, sinning, or dishonoring God. Thankfully, we have the same Spirit of Jesus living inside us now!

Our flesh (our default sinful nature) is very much like Esau and wants to react in sinful ways when we are in raw moments. But the Holy Spirit inside us wants to be like Jesus and **choose** faithfulness.

**So part of becoming more like Jesus is making decisions in the raw moments like Jesus.** The Holy Spirit provides us **the opportunity to make a choice** with what we do in our hunger, anger, loneliness, etc.

## JOURNAL

**We all have raw moments.** Are there some people you've sinned against recently while you were in a raw moment? Have you apologized and tried to make things right with them? Find time to do so today.

**Being raw typically happens when we are angry, hungry, lonely, afraid, stressed, or sad.** Which of these raw moments do you need to be most careful of? Are you especially prone to act foolishly with any of them in particular? How so?

**Jacob took advantage of his brother's vulnerability.** Have you done this recently? Manipulated someone's weakness to get something from them? Taken advantage of someone because they are not thinking clearly? Are you holding bitterness or a grudge against someone who sinned against you when they were vulnerable? Take some time to repent of those things if you have.

**Jesus used Scripture to help Him stay faithful when He was raw.** What Scripture can you use to help you in your raw moments? Have you memorized them to help? Commit to memorizing them if you haven't. If Jesus did it, we should probably also!

### CLOSING PRAYER

*"Jesus, You experienced the same things I do when it comes to raw moments. Please help me choose You over my flesh in those times. May I love people well even when I am angry, tired, sad, stressed, or hungry. Please give me the courage to apologize to those I need to apologize to. I love You. Amen!"*

# 19

# Isaac's Family Implodes

## OPENING PRAYER

*"Hello, Jesus. Lord, I pray that You would bless this time together. May I hear what You have for me today. Please give me what I need today and help me to receive it gratefully. You are so good to me. I love You, Lord. Amen."*

## SCRIPTURE

Genesis 27:1–28:9

## THINK

- *Where is His grace?*
- *Where is His lordship?*
- *This family has fallen apart, and everyone is to blame. What sins against each other do you see? What sins against God do you see? Go through each individually: Jacob, Esau, Rebekah, Isaac.*

## READ

Watching this family fall apart can be hard to watch. Isaac and Rebekah play favorites with their kids. Rebekah and Jacob deceive blind Isaac. Isaac basically "trades" the blessing for a meal (like Esau did to Jacob in our last story). Esau threatens Jacob's life. Jacob doesn't repent but runs from his problems and will sadly never see his mother again. It's a mess, and everyone is to blame.

This is the family God has chosen to work with. And the crazy part is that He still chooses to work with them. Despite their brokenness, their sin, and their personalities, God is still present and will fulfill His promises. He will use broken people to accomplish His will. And the reality is that in Jesus, we are welcomed into a new family...

## SCRIPTURE

Galatians 3:25–29

## READ

This passage tells us that God *doesn't* show favoritism in His family. Not between Jew or Gentile (non-Jew), slave or free, male or female...we are all loved by Him! **God is in the business of family-*building*.** Yes, this partially refers to your immediate blood-family, but when you become a Christian, you are part of the family of believers.

God calls this the church. (The word "church" is never used in the Bible to refer to a building. It is *always* the followers of Jesus.) You become more related by Jesus' blood than to your own family by blood. **This is why Christians are called to live in community together as the church. It's for building and expanding God's family.**

But if you haven't noticed already, God's family is sometimes filled with people like Isaac's family. The church sadly can be greedy, selfish, deceitful, and sometimes dangerous. (If it's physically dangerous or filled with false teachings from the leadership, you should definitely not be a part of that local church!)

Maybe you've had bad experiences from churches, and you don't want anything to do with God's family anymore. It's totally understandable, and yet God tells us that we are *still* a part of it. If you struggle with being a part of a local church, try remembering a few things...

First, this is something God calls us to invest in as He invests in us. To walk alone with Jesus is to not walk with Him. Being with His people is essential.

Second, the church will *always* be filled with imperfect people. Everyone is at different stages in their walk with God, so we need to be gracious and encouraging to each other as we try to follow Jesus as best as we can (Hebrews 10:24–25). As God has forgiven us, we should forgive others.

Third, check your own heart. Have *you* needed to change your attitude and mindset regarding the church? What role have *you* played in your own experience?

When you go to be with the church this week (or if you don't go, try to find a way to), try to be really present. These people are part of your family. Take some small steps. Try to meet someone, remembering they are your brother or sister in Jesus. Pay attention to the sermon. Worship with all your might. You being fully present makes God's family stronger!

Maybe you already love being part of your local church. That's great! Then keep going. Double-down on what you are learning and practicing so that *when* (not if) struggles in the church happen, you are equipped to handle it well.

## JOURNAL

**Isaac and Rebekah sinned by playing favorites.** Do you play favorites with your kids? Employees? Do you tend to bless those who are more like you than those who aren't? Do you give special privileges to those you like while treating others unfairly? Do you consider someone's worth to be based on their accomplishments or personality rather than being an image-bearer of God?

**Esau had married two Canaanite women that his parents didn't approve of in Genesis 26:34–35.** He then tries to win his parents' affections by marrying a daughter of Ishmael, sinning again by marrying *another* woman and one who didn't follow God at that. Sometimes we are tempted to sin in order to win our parents' love. Maybe we act out in rebellion, try to be perfect, or always try to read their minds to gain their approval. Are there any ways you are putting your parents' approval over God's? Are you ruled by seeking their blessing rather than trying to please God? Who has more power over your actions and thoughts?

## CLOSING PRAYER

*"Dad, sometimes being part of Your family is hard. There are a lot of imperfect people, but I'm one of them too. Please teach me how to be a good sibling to my Christian brothers and sisters. Please help me pay attention and be fully present next Sunday. Amen!"*

# 20

# Jacob's Wives

## OPENING PRAYER

*"Dear Lord, thank You again for this time together. Thank You for the work You have been doing in my heart and mind. Would You continue that work in me today? I want to be more like You, Jesus. Even though it's hard to see change in me sometimes, I trust You are doing good things. Thank You! I love You so much!"*

## SCRIPTURE

Genesis 29:1–30

## THINK

- *Where is His grace?*
- *Where is His lordship?*
- *Is there anything here we've seen before?*
- *What might God be doing in the background of this story?*

## READ

This story is almost a flip of Abraham's servant finding Rebekah. Instead of a godly man Abraham trusted, we've got an ungodly deceiver in Jacob. Where the servant prays that God would lead him to a godly woman, Jacob doesn't seek God at all and instead goes all in on a woman he thinks is pretty.

Now, we've met Jacob's Uncle Laban before. He was eyeing all of the servant's riches when he came for his sister, Rebekah. He's greedy to have Jacob work for him and swaps out the blessing of Rachel at the last minute for his firstborn, Leah. (Sound a bit similar to our last story?)

Now here's the thing. Jacob didn't love Leah and yet he was married to her. Though incredibly sad and hard, Jacob's feelings about the situation should not have mattered. If he was a godly man, he would have committed fully to Leah and tried to be the best husband he could be for her, just as God commits to us in all of our imperfections. But instead, he decides to be like Lamech and marry Rachel also!

Just like Lamech, Jacob **SAW** this woman, **CONSIDERED HER GOOD**, and **TOOK** her as a second wife. Today, our culture would be applauding him for following his heart: *"He has a right to do this. It was true love! It's not loving to Leah if he doesn't love her, so he should just let her go marry someone else."* But that's not true love in God's eyes.

Instead of investing in his marriage to Leah, Jacob wastes seven years of his life working for a woman who isn't his wife! How devastating is that for Leah?

We won't read the following chapters in this study, but Rachel and Leah's relationship will be completely broken also. They're going to compete for Jacob's love by trying to have as many kids as possible. It gets so bad that they have Jacob sleep with their servants, Bilhah and Zilpah, in order to have more kids (Genesis 29–30). Can you imagine being one of those kids in that family? It's a complete disaster.

Fortunately, we worship a God who is the exact opposite of Jacob...

## SCRIPTURE

Luke 23:1–16

## READ

This story takes place as Jesus is being handed over to be crucified. He goes through a sham trial, and then the Pharisees convince Pilate to kill Jesus even though He was innocent. But why does Jesus go through this injustice? Out of love for His bride, the church.

Jacob suffered injustice from Uncle Laban, but instead of pursuing his bride, he pursued another woman who was more beautiful to him. (We know nothing of Rachel's character.) **But Jesus suffered injustice _in order_ to be with His bride, beautiful but not of good character.**

Even though we sin and are broken, Jesus went through injustice to not only be with us, but also to bring us full, fruitful lives. Jacob should have focused on bringing a full, fruitful life to Leah as her husband, but he didn't.

In the same way, Jesus calls us to commit to Him as our one "spouse." As followers of Jesus, we don't work seven years for Jesus and then work seven years for what we actually want. No, Jesus becomes what we want, and we spend all our energy pouring into our relationship with _Him_.

Maybe it's hard to see Jesus as beautiful at times. But the more we spend time with Him, learn about Him, and experience Him, over time we won't be able to help but see Him as beautiful, amazing, and incredible.

Satan wants to deceive us like Uncle Laban did. He'll encourage us to put our efforts into "a new bride" instead of Jesus. Something that seems more attractive, more fun, more life-giving, more fulfilling, more promising...we must be on guard. May Christ be our model, not Jacob.

## JOURNAL

**When we love things, it's not a bad thing.** It's only bad when we make a good thing a "god." In other words, we are not to put our whole identity and value into something other than our first love, Jesus. What are some things you are putting before your relationship with Jesus? Grades? Popularity? Work? Family? Kids? Grandkids? Money? Career? Home? Reputation?

**Jacob wasted years of his life in order to gain something ungodly and devastating, though to him in the moment, it seemed wonderful.** Have you experienced this? Is there anything you are chasing now that may very well destroy your life? Are there any areas where you are wearing "rose-colored glasses" and not seeing things clearly, especially when it comes to a romantic relationship? Ask someone you trust to share if they see this in you.

**Jacob the deceiver was deceived.** Sometimes God uses irony in our lives to get our attention. Has He done this in your life? Is there any hypocrisy He is trying to expose in You?

## CLOSING PRAYER

*"Jesus, thank You for being faithful and committed to me. May I be faithful and committed to You first. I love You. Amen."*

# 21

# Jacob Wrestles God

## OPENING PRAYER

*"Dear Lord, I love You. May I love You more. I enjoy You. May I enjoy You more. I am thankful for You. May I be more thankful for You. I praise You. May I praise You more. Would You please use this time for Your glory and my benefit? Amen!"*

## READ

Jacob is more than a fascinating character in the Bible. He was a real, living, breathing person. And he changed and grew over time. Did he ever become perfect? No. **But what we do see is growth.**

We're going to look at three stories of Jacob encountering God in two special places. Maybe there's a place that's special to you where you encountered God. But each time Jacob goes back to this place, he has grown.

This first story is a rewind—it's after he steals Esau's birthright from Isaac and leaves home and before he meets Rachel...

## SCRIPTURE

Genesis 28:10–22

## THINK

- *Where is His grace?*
- *Where is His lordship?*

## READ

Jacob had just done something terrible but now has this incredible vision from God. He hears God's voice and His promise for his life. The Abrahamic Covenant that was passed on to Isaac has now been passed on to him.

Jacob has a "spiritual high" and makes promises to God about having a relationship with Him. Maybe you've had a moment like that. Perhaps it happened at a summer camp, a worship service, or a missions trip. God felt incredibly real to you, and you committed your life to Him.

But then things got in the way. You sort of forgot about the things of God or pushed it off to the side. Jacob will do the exact same thing with his shenanigans with Rachel, Leah, and Uncle Laban. Though Jacob is praising God, his faith is far from mature.

In this next story, Jacob is returning home to where Isaac lives. But on the way back home, he encounters God again...

## SCRIPTURE

Genesis 32:22–32

## THINK

- *Where is His grace?*
- *Where is His lordship?*

## READ

Jacob has always been willing to do whatever it takes to get what he wants. And we see it again here when he tries to win a wrestling match *after* his hip has been miraculously dislocated.

He has been a manipulator his whole life. He got Esau to do what he wanted, Isaac to do what he wanted, Uncle Laban to do what he wanted...and it even appears he's getting this mysterious man to do what he wanted: bless him.

But once he realizes *who* he's been wrestling, he realizes *he* was the one being shown mercy. Something clicks inside Jacob, causing him to realize he can't manipulate God. Ever.

Yes, God tells him that he won the fight. And yes, God does bless him. But it's not because Jacob won the fight. It's because he's part of God's plan.

God is refocusing Jacob's stubbornness away from selfishness and towards obedience. It's taken a while for Jacob to get there, but he's progressing.

It's here God renames Jacob "Israel," which means "wrestles with God." This will prove highly symbolic of God's relationship with the nation of Israel as a whole.

God ends up permanently injuring Jacob, reminding Him who's really in charge. God may do this with us still. If we are stubborn against

God, He may give us a challenge to remind us that ultimately He is in control and His direction is the way we should stubbornly go.

## SCRIPTURE

Genesis 35:1–15

## THINK

- *Where is His grace?*
- *Where is His lordship?*

## READ

God tells Jacob to return to the place where he had the vision of the ladder all those years ago. And Jacob obeys. He's been humbled, been injured, and made a mess of things. And yet, God promises to bless and use him.

Jacob removes all the foreign gods that his family acquired over the years and builds an altar to worship God. He has finally matured in his faith.

Jacob is going to continue to make terrible decisions and, tragically, will play favorites with his own sons. But we have to acknowledge the slow progress of Jacob's life towards God. He grows.

## SCRIPTURE

Romans 7:18–25

## READ

Paul recognizes here that we are all going to wrestle with sin, God, our flesh…it's part of life. **While we are all going to wrestle, it's not an excuse to sin.**

But the question becomes, **"Are you wrestling *towards* God or fighting *against* Him?"**

Wrestling towards God means we are struggling *in order to* trust and obey Him more. Fighting against God means we are struggling *to get away from* His authority in our lives. We are called to wrestle towards Him, even when it is messy.

Because Jesus took the judgment of sin, we are free to *grow stronger* through wrestling rather than fighting for God's approval. This is good news! It means we can rejoice in our progress and growth rather than beat ourselves up for not being good enough! Praise God!

## JOURNAL

**Think about your relationship with God this past year.** What are some ways you have grown? Really take your time with this. Write them out and praise God for helping you grow!

**A purpose of the church is to build each other up.** Ask someone who knows you well how they have seen you grow in your faith. Write those things down and reflect on them. Praise God for them. Then reach out to others and encourage them by sharing how you've seen them grow.

**Jacob set up pillars to remind himself of what God has done.** If you are journaling, you can consider your entries as pillars. Read back through some of your journal entries and praise God for what

*He* has been doing in and through you. Are there other ways you can place reminders of His faithfulness around you? Pictures? Post-it notes? Artwork? Memorabilia? The more prompts you have around you to remind you of how faithful God is, the better!

## CLOSING PRAYER

*"Jesus, thank You for the ways You have taught me this past year. May I continue to grow and rejoice in You. May I not be discouraged in my sinfulness but instead be thankful that You are with me to help me. I love You so much! Amen!"*

# 22

# Joseph the "Golden Child"

## OPENING PRAYER

*"Jesus, you are so good to me. On earth you were an obedient Son to the Father. I want to be like You. Would you help me see YOU as my role model. Even though I may have some heroes, none of them are as great as You. Please change my heart to see and know that. I love You. Amen."*

## SCRIPTURE

Genesis 37

## THINK

- *Where is His grace?*
- *Where is His lordship?*
- *We've been following this family for a while now. What patterns have you seen in the family dynamics? Patterns with God?*

## READ

Meet Joseph: the "golden child." Now at first glance, it may seem that Joseph was a good kid who was a victim of evil. And though he certainly was a victim, we do see some big character flaws in this young man.

Twice Joseph shares his prophetic dreams with brothers who hate him about his family bowing down to him. Was Joseph oblivious to their hatred? Probably not. Brothers tend not to be subtle. More likely, he was taking these dreams from God and flaunting it in their faces.

We also see him working with his brothers and bringing a bad report about them to their father. Notice how Joseph doesn't work with them after that? Instead, Jacob uses him as a tattletale on their behavior.

And what does Joseph do while getting this report? He wears an incredibly beautiful robe his dad gave him as the favorite. I have a hard time believing this wasn't on purpose. In later stories, we will see that Joseph is incredibly competent, smart, and self-aware.

Maybe you have a sibling who is the golden child in your family. They're just perfect and never do anything wrong (or no one notices when they do!). Maybe you're like the brothers, jealous of his praise.

Or maybe *you* are the golden child! Maybe you feel the weight of pressure to be perfect and never mess up. Maybe you've let things get to your head, leading you to believe that no one is as good as you. Maybe you've abused it to make your life better.

Healthy families don't play favorites, but this one sure did. Jacob's sinfulness leads him to love Joseph more than his other kids. But Joseph's pride and his brothers' jealousy make things worse!

Remember, broken relationships are often broken in both directions. There's usually blame on both sides, so it is important that we analyze *our* actions and not just those who hurt us.

Even though Joseph heard from God correctly, the *way* he went about it was not only unwise but prideful. **It is possible for us to handle the truths of God incorrectly and even evilly.**

Our families are supposed to be our biggest supporters. They are supposed to challenge and encourage us. God intended family to be a godly support structure to help us grow up to be more like Him. A safe place where we can make mistakes, forgive each other, and become more like Jesus together.

Maybe you have a family like this: one that pushes you closer to Jesus. If so, PRAISE GOD! Be humble and grateful for that! And seek to love your family really well.

But maybe that's not the case in your family. Maybe there are tense relationships, hurt, pain, rivalries, jealousies, and comparison. Our relationships are not meant to be that way. And even if you try to be a good sibling, son/daughter, spouse, parent...maybe others aren't trying. Jesus knows what it's like to not have that support structure.

## SCRIPTURE

Matthew 26:36–56

## READ

Jesus was going through His biggest trial ever. And He wanted His "brothers" (the disciples) to be with Him in it. They aren't blood-related, but they are who Jesus spent the most time with. (In John 7:5, we learn Jesus' real-life blood brothers did not yet believe in Him.)

Jesus asks them to pray for and encourage Him, and they end up falling asleep. And here, not only did His family abandon Him to go through the crucifixion alone, but one of them even betrays Him. And later, Peter will deny ever knowing Jesus.

Now Jesus knew this was going to happen. He predicted Peter's denial, Judas' betrayal, and the disciples abandoning Him. But just because He was prepared for it didn't mean that it didn't hurt.

So if you are in a family that doesn't pursue Jesus like you do or one that is filled with brokenness, you can take comfort knowing that Jesus knows how that feels. He is with you. He feels for you. And You are not alone.

## JOURNAL

**Both Joseph and Jesus experienced betrayal.** Have you ever felt betrayed or hurt by someone really close to you? What was that like? How did it make you feel? When you read about Jesus also experiencing betrayal and hurt, how does that make you feel? Does it change anything for you?

**Joseph had received prophetic dreams but responded to them poorly.** Have you ever done that with a prophetic dream or a truth from God? Do you brag about your blessings? Do you speak too much? Do you constantly feel the need to share *everything* with people? Do you not have a filter or take time to consider how your words might be received? Take time asking God to empower you with self-control over your mouth.

**Joseph and his brothers responded to their father's favoritism in different ways.** Joseph leveraged it to get away with things. His brothers responded with hatred and jealousy. In your family, have you responded to favoritism like this before? Do you still? How about in your job or class? Are *you* the "golden" co-worker or student? How do you respond to the "favorites" in your setting?

## CLOSING PRAYER

*"Father, thank You for being with me. Please help me be wise and loving in my relationships. May I respond as a beloved child of You in all I do. May I live today knowing You are with me. I love You. Amen."*

23

# Joseph & Potiphar's Wife

## OPENING PRAYER

*"Dear God, I thank You for helping me have time for this study today. I desire to know and love You more. Please empower me to grow in my knowledge and understanding of You. Amen."*

## SCRIPTURE

Genesis 39

## THINK

- *Where is His grace?*
- *Where is His lordship?*
- *How much does Joseph's character play a factor in this story?*

## READ

Joseph went from a prideful boy who apparently didn't do much work to a humble man who became the best worker. His character grew tremendously. We saw hints of it when Joseph responded *"Here I am"* to his father…it's a phrase many faithful people say throughout Scripture. But here we see remarkable growth.

The difference-maker for Joseph was God's presence working inside and through him. Only God could do that sort of work in someone.

Now of course Joseph's work and character had a big role to play, but the Bible is clear that *God's* work and character was the *real* reason why he had success everywhere. God's faithfulness to Joseph, working alongside Joseph's growing humility and work ethic, led to Joseph being in a position of blessing in Potiphar's household.

Joseph was completely trustworthy because God was completely trustworthy. It's probably the reason why Potiphar didn't kill Joseph after his wife's accusation and only throws him in prison. He probably sensed that she was lying because the Joseph he knew would never do something so wrong. **See, being good at what you do has some importance. Who you are is of more importance. And who you worship has the most importance.**

Success can sometimes inspire others, but oftentimes it leads to jealousy and unhealthy admiration. Potiphar's wife **SAW** Joseph, **CONSIDERED HIM GOOD**, and attempted to **TAKE** him for herself. In a way, she is like Eve offering the fruit to Adam for him to eat. She is committed to sinning against God and her husband and then invites Joseph to do the same.

But Joseph does the opposite of what Adam does. He runs in the opposite direction! **And he has to keep running from her, because she keeps pursuing him!**

Sin is relentless in its pursuit over us, and we are called to obey every time. Joseph has seen what affairs and terrible marriages can result in firsthand. He realizes he doesn't have to live like them and wants to glorify God instead.

## SCRIPTURE

Matthew 26:57–68

## READ

Joseph is sold by his own family (Israelites) to a rival family (Ishmaelites) and then to an enemy nation (Egypt). Similarly, Jesus was sold by his own family (Jews) and killed unjustly by an enemy nation (Rome). **Joseph, a near perfect employee, was lied about and falsely put in prison. Jesus, a perfect person, was lied about and falsely sentenced to death.**

The sad reality of life is that there will be times when doing the right thing will result in unjust results. Our world is broken. Life isn't fair. We shouldn't expect it to be. Yes, we should and are called by God to seek justice in all circumstances. But we need to have a realistic picture of the world alongside that.

That's why it's so important for us to put our faith in Jesus for the New Heaven and New Earth. Life will be fair then, but only then. There will be no injustice, no sin, and no temptation to sin.

When we are wronged, we can mourn (like Jesus) and seek justice (as Jesus told us to). But our future hope should give us courage and strength in the middle of it. We don't need to be surprised when the world is just being the world. **We can be mourners of injustice, pursuers of justice, and celebrators of God's coming freedom all at the same time.**

## JOURNAL

**God's blessing through Joseph's character and work ethic brought blessing to all those around him.** Do you know anyone God does that through? Does He do it in your own life? Do you have the reputation of having God's hand on you? Are there any ways you may be preventing God from working through you? Where are some areas where you have had success? How did your **work ethic** contribute to your success? How did your **character** contribute? And how did **God** contribute?

**Both Joseph and Jesus were condemned when they did the right thing.** Have you ever experienced injustice when you were doing the right thing? Did you respond like Jesus/Joseph? Have you ever punished someone for doing the right thing? Perhaps got back at someone for telling the truth about a wrong you did?

**The world will always have injustice until Jesus returns and makes all things right.** How might that be an encouragement in your life? Your family's life? Your friends' lives?

## CLOSING PRAYER

*"Jesus, thank You for showing me what it looks like to endure injustice. May I be someone who endures injustice well. May I be a light and testimony of Your success in me even when circumstances are falling apart. I love You, Jesus. Amen."*

24

# The Cupbearer & the Baker

## OPENING PRAYER

*"Lord, You are always there for me, even when I forget. You have placed people in my life to be there for. You have given me people to love intentionally. May I love people well today. Would You please teach me how to love others better? Amen!"*

## SCRIPTURE

Genesis 40

## THINK

- *Where is His grace?*
- *Where is His lordship?*
- *How has Joseph matured when it comes to prophetic dreams?*

## Read

Joseph sees his fellow prisoners having a tough day and checks in on them. There was something about Joseph's character that made him sensitive to those around him. This is a great attribute that not all of us have, but one that we should all foster.

He asks and then offers to help. He doesn't force them but invites them to share only if they are comfortable. And when they do share, he listens. This is an incredible model of friendship.

Joseph **offers** to bless the baker (by listening to his story). The baker **accepts** the offer to share and **listens** to Joseph's answer. Then Joseph tells him the **truth**.

Joseph had to give the baker some bad news. The baker was going to receive the wrath of Pharaoh. Joseph didn't sugarcoat it. He didn't lie to him. He didn't try to make him feel better. He told the baker the reality of his situation in the context of love.

There are people who haven't given their lives to Jesus yet. Like the baker, these friends are in danger of receiving God's wrath. They aren't yet in "right standing" with God.

Maybe you are the person God wants to use to tell them the bad news so that they can understand the good news of Jesus. Like Joseph, **you will need to seek God's leading on the timing and the words to say**. And when/if He does lead you to share the good news about Jesus to them, you need to tell the truth. If that intimidates you, ask someone further along in their faith for wisdom on how to go about it.

Remember the context of Joseph's words though. **He had a *relationship* with the baker before he told him the truth about his situation.** He tried to be a good friend *first*. He asked and listened and sought to bless him *before* telling him the hard news. So before you tell your friend the hard news about the wrath of God and good news about Jesus, try to love this friend to the best of your ability first.

## SCRIPTURE

Mark 9:14–29

## READ

Jesus didn't have to ask the boy's father how long he had been possessed by an evil spirit. He already knew. But Jesus took the time to listen to the father's story.

**Jesus didn't want to just solve this father's problem. He wanted to really *love* him *while* solving his problem.** He wanted the father to feel heard, known, and understood. He is a friend who listens.

But here's what is important for us to see. ***God* is the one who addresses the problems of both the father and the prisoners.** Jesus is the one who casts out the demon. God is the one who gives Joseph the interpretation of the dream. Joseph says he can't do it without God's help. We should have the same attitude. **Our friends need *God's* help. We need *His* leading to show us *how* to love our friends well.**

Maybe you are someone who is more oblivious to how those around you are feeling. God values feelings and so should we. Take this as a charge to be more aware and in touch with the feelings of others.

Maybe you're someone who tries to solve everyone's problems when you are not asked. We can always offer, but we need to make sure that the other person *wants* our help. Take this as a charge to slow down, listen, and humble yourself. Don't presume you automatically know the solution to someone's problem. It's arrogant.

Maybe you're someone who's not great at listening. You stop paying attention or maybe you are so focused on your own response that you're not hearing them anymore. Don't seek to help with a problem you *think* they are having, but seek to *understand* their problem first. Take this as a charge to truly love someone by giving them your full, undivided attention.

## JOURNAL

**Joseph's character, his ability to love, and God's blessing over his life led others to be vulnerable with him.** Do people feel comfortable being vulnerable with you? Do people come to you for wisdom? Advice? Insight? Prayer? Encouragement? Why? Why not? Is there anything you are doing now that keeps people from coming to you? Are you oblivious? Insensitive? Quick to judge? Quick to speak and slow to listen? Take courage to ask someone to assess you in this area, listen humbly, and ask God for help so that you may love people better.

**Jesus listens well.** How often do you take time to really pour out your heart to Jesus? Are you comfortable being vulnerable with Him? Do you consistently go to Him? Do you provide space to be comforted by Him? Or do you speak your piece and hurry on to the next thing? Do you provide time for Him to speak into your concerns? Take some time to do so now.

## CLOSING PRAYER

*"Jesus, You are my Best Friend. Would You please teach me and shape me to be a great friend to those around me. May I love my friends by serving them and by having the wisdom and courage to tell them the hard truth. May I listen and love well like You do. I love you, Lord. Amen."*

# 25

# Joseph Rises to Power

## OPENING PRAYER

*"Lord, Your timing is perfect. I don't always understand why You do things when You do them. You work at a pace different than mine. Would You help me to trust Your timing in my life so I can live with more peace and trust in You. Amen."*

## SCRIPTURE

Genesis 41

## THINK

- *Where is His grace?*
- *Where is His lordship?*
- *Who is God revealing Himself to? How?*

## READ

FINALLY! After all these years, Joseph finally learns what God was doing in His life. God used Joseph to save lives by placing him in a position of power...

after giving Joseph a dream...

after using Joseph's arrogance to stir his brothers' anger...

after sparing Joseph from their wrath...

after moving Joseph unjustly to prison...

after giving Joseph the interpretation of the cupbearer's dream...

after giving Pharaoh a dream...

after reminding the cupbearer of Joseph...

All of it on purpose.

God had been orchestrating every single moment. Every mistake, every unjust action, every victory, every loss, every relationship...God used it all to accomplish His goals.

He is the One *truly* in charge of our lives. And He is *wise* in how He does everything. Look at how much we can trust Him with our own lives when things don't turn out the way we want them to!

And not only that, but God was preparing Joseph's character along the way. Joseph started out as an obnoxious, selfish, spoiled brat who bragged about being better than everyone else. And by the time this opportunity with Pharaoh happened, he was a humble, hard-working man who wanted the best for those around him. Even Pharaoh admitted he had never met someone like Joseph. What a change!

God's timing was perfect in his life for both the work He wanted done *through* Joseph and the work He wanted to get done *in* Joseph.

At the beginning, Joseph thought the vision was all about himself becoming great. But after a long time of God showing Joseph who was really in charge of his life, Joseph's mind about greatness changed. God brought greatness to Joseph so that he could serve and save lives. In a much greater way, Jesus did the same thing...

## SCRIPTURE

Philippians 2:5–8
Matthew 20:25–28

## READ

Joseph needed to learn that greatness, power, and influence are meant to be used to serve others. Jesus didn't. His goal is always to serve others.

It's normal to think the more successful you are, the more praise and privilege you deserve. But Jesus proves that the opposite is correct. The more successful and great you are, the more you are called to lay down your life and serve others.

Jesus became helpless to help those who arrested Him.

Jesus gave up His privileges of being King so that we may become heirs of God.

Jesus gave up His power so we may be empowered by the Holy Spirit.

Jesus gave up His earthly life to give us eternal life.

Jesus' sacrifices give us more than we could ever get!

Joseph was betrayed, sold, falsely accused, and arrested, all outside of his own desires. Jesus was betrayed, sold, falsely accused, arrested, *and killed* by His own desire to obey the Father.

Joseph was exalted to become second in command to save the world from earthly hunger. Jesus was exalted to become King and save the world from earthly *and* spiritual hunger for all of eternity.

## JOURNAL

**It is natural for us to want to become great.** God calls us to be hard-working, set goals, try our best, and seek success (take a look through Proverbs to learn more). But He cares about our hearts and attitudes as we do it. What are some areas of your life where you would like to be great? Do you want that greatness because you want praise, recognition, power, and privilege? Or do you want it to honor God and serve others?

**Joseph was in the dark about what God was doing for most of his life.** He was sold into slavery at age seventeen and became second in command of Egypt at age thirty. Do you feel in the dark about what God is doing in your life? How are you responding to it? What's your attitude? What have your prayers sounded like? Any patterns? Any patterns that need to change? Has God brought you any clarity through Scripture?

**The names of Joseph's sons reveal his heart towards God.** Take time to consider the ways God has turned things around in your life. Ways He has brought good out of evil. Ways He has saved and transformed your life. Take time to thank and praise Him for those things.

## CLOSING PRAYER

*"Jesus, I am amazed at how You chose me to display Your greatness and power. May I have the same mind and heart as You. May I not try to build up myself. May I not seek fame or recognition, but only Your glory in all I do. May people see my life and think of You. To You only be the glory today. Amen."*

# 26

# Joseph & His Brothers Reunite

## OPENING PRAYER

*"Dear God, Your ways can be mysterious. There are many times when You do things that I do not understand. May I become okay with not needing to understand it all. May I simply walk and trust You more today than I did yesterday. Would You please bless this time together? Amen."*

## READ

Genesis 42–47 explain at length the dramatic story of Joseph reuniting with his brothers. I encourage you to read it, but for this study we will hone in on only a couple of chapters. To summarize what leads up to today's reading...

The famine that Pharaoh dreamed about comes to pass. Jacob hears that there is food in Egypt, so he sends Joseph's ten older brothers to buy food to save their lives.

When they arrive, Joseph sees them, but they don't recognize him. (It's been at least twenty years since they've seen him, and he is dressed as an Egyptian ruler.) Angry and suspicious of them, Joseph accuses them of being spies. They deny it, so he decides to put them to the test.

He sends them back to Jacob with food but imprisons one of his brothers, Simeon. He tells the rest that if they want to free him, they must bring back Benjamin, the second son of Jacob's favorite wife, Rachel.

The brothers return to Jacob who at first refuses, not wanting to risk Benjamin's life. But when they run out of food again, he agrees. They bring Benjamin to Joseph, and Simeon is set free. But the test isn't over...

## SCRIPTURE

Genesis 44:1–45:10
Genesis 50:14–21

## THINK

- *Where is His grace?*
- *Where is His lordship?*
- *What might the brothers be feeling throughout this experience?*

## READ

Look at how Joseph described his life to his brothers. He recognizes that it was God who brought him to power for their benefit! He acknowledges that God used their evil actions to save them and thousands of others.

Because of his understanding of God's sovereignty and grace, Joseph is able to forgive his brothers, not holding any of their evil against them. Jesus did the same to an even greater extent...

## SCRIPTURE

Luke 23:33–38
Romans 8:28

## READ

**Joseph forgave his brothers after they had completed their evil. Jesus forgave us while we still do evil.**

Joseph told his brothers not to fear his wrath. They have already been forgiven. Jesus invites us to take that same courage.

If God has already forgiven us and will always use it for good, then can't we do whatever we want? He are some thoughts...

**First**, think about how much damage the brothers did. Jacob was heartbroken for over twenty years thinking his son was dead. The brothers lived with guilt for over twenty years. Benjamin didn't grow up with his older brother. There are always real-life consequences to our actions.

**Second**, yes, in some very real ways you are still "allowed" to sin. That's what forgiveness is. But how does that benefit your relationship with God? Forgiveness is meant to lead to a stronger relationship with Him. Why would you *want* to hurt that relationship?

**Third**, if you *want* to keep sinning, it may indicate that you aren't repentant or saved in the first place. True followers of Jesus battle the tension between sinning and obeying God, but if you'd rather just keep sinning, it may prove you aren't in a real relationship with God.

**Fourth**, Jesus says we will receive rewards in heaven based on what we do on earth (Matthew 25:14–30). Building His Kingdom, sharing the gospel, blessing and serving others...all those things bring rewards in

Heaven (1 Corinthians 3:10–15). But if you are sinning on purpose and undermining your effectiveness for God, you're not only wasting your life on things that don't matter, but you're also keeping yourself from gaining eternal rewards. That's foolish!

## JOURNAL

**Joseph tested his brothers to see where their hearts were.** God will often do the same to either expose sin we need to repent of or to encourage us in Him. Reflecting on your life, what are some tests you've passed well? Tests you've failed? Are you in one now? What is being revealed to you?

**God used the evil and foolishness of Joseph's brothers to do good.** When was a time God has used your foolishness or sin to do good for others? When are some times when your sin has had bad consequences on those around you? Take some time to praise Him for being merciful to you.

**Joseph was able to forgive because of the perspective God had given him.** Are you withholding forgiveness from anyone? If so, what perspective might you be lacking? What makes forgiveness so hard? How was Jesus able to forgive? How might you?

## CLOSING PRAYER

*"Lord, Your forgiveness can be confusing and hard to understand sometimes. Sometimes it is hard for me to believe that You have fully forgiven me and that I don't have to live in shame. Please help me live in the confidence of Your mercy and goodness over my life. Amen."*

THE EXODUS ERA

# PART III: THE EXODUS ERA

## SUMMARY

*God delivers a nation out of slavery, calling them to be His people and a shining beacon of hope to a dark world.*

## THE SCRIPTURE OF THIS ERA

Exodus
Leviticus
Numbers
Deuteronomy

## INTRODUCTION

In our last era, God initiated a special relationship with Abraham, Isaac, Jacob, and his descendants bound by the **Abrahamic Covenant**. As a reminder, this incorporated three promises from God:

1. He would build Abraham into a nation.
2. He would give that nation a land.
3. He would bless the world through that nation.

We followed this dysfunctional family through the generations, watching God work through both their good and evil to accomplish His purposes. The Patriarch Era ends with Jacob, his twelve sons, and their families living in Egypt under Joseph's protection with the Pharaoh's blessing—seventy people in all (Genesis 46:27). Not yet a nation, but well on its way.

Back when God confirmed this covenant with Abraham in Genesis 15:18–21, He tells him the exact plot of land He intends to give His people: *"from the river of Egypt to the great river, the river Euphrates, the land of the Kenites, the Kenizzites, the Kadmonites, the Hittites, the Perizzites, the Rephaim, the Amorites, the Canaanites, the Girgashites, and the Jebusites."*

But it's not time for them to have the land yet. God explains why in verse 16: *"And [your descendants] shall come back here in the fourth generation, for the iniquity of the Amorites is not yet complete."*

The Amorites, Canaanites, and others listed were wicked nations God was intending to judge for their evil. (We'll cover this more in our next era.) He will send Abraham's descendants to take the land, but in the interim, God reveals in verses 13–14 that his *"offspring will be sojourners in a land that is not theirs and will be servants there, and they will be afflicted for four hundred years. But I will bring judgment on the nation that they serve, and afterward they shall come out with great possessions."*

It's in this affliction that the **Exodus Era** begins. It follows the plight of the Hebrew people and their miraculous deliverance by God through Moses from the Egyptians—thus the title "Exodus," which refers to a departure of a large group of people. (The term "Hebrews" refers to the descendants of Abraham.) They will make a covenant with God at Mt. Sinai and wander through the wilderness towards the land God promised them until rebellion keeps them from taking it.

# 27

# Pharaoh & the Midwives

## OPENING PRAYER

*"God, thank You for being with me in this journey of reading through Your word. Thank You for the work You have been doing in me already. Please continue to teach me and bring me closer to You. I love You, Lord! Amen!"*

## SCRIPTURE

Exodus 1

## THINK

- *Where is His grace?*
- *Where is His lordship?*

## READ

God's promise to Abraham to build a nation is coming to fruition as the Hebrew people were *"fruitful and multiplied."* Hopefully this reminded you of God's commands to Adam and Eve and to Noah. God is in the business of expanding His good Kingdom through His people.

It is in the midst of God's blessing where a new antagonist arises: Pharaoh. According to his religion, he would have considered himself a god. He has his own kingdom. **Where God desires to multiply His people in order to bless the world, Pharaoh wants to stifle the Hebrews to maintain his world.**

But as we see here, nothing will stop God from completing His work. Neither hard labor nor slavery can prevent God from multiplying His people. And so Pharaoh does something that sets a ticking clock to his nation's destruction and judgment from God.

He commits a genocide of all the Hebrew baby boys, preventing them from growing up to become strong men who could rise up in rebellion against him.

God takes it seriously when children are murdered.

Very seriously.

Ironically, there will be five *women* listed in this chapter and the next who display incredible courage, paving the way towards the Hebrews' deliverance.

The first two are Shiphrah and Puah, the midwives. They are perhaps two of the most courageous women in the Bible. They feared God more than Pharaoh. They knew who was the true God and who had the true power. And in order to obey God, they deceive Pharaoh.

*"Isn't lying a sin?"* Well, we are going to learn something very important about God here.

As we grow up, we are often taught to do the right thing. *"Don't do this. Do this. Don't do that. Do that. Don't go here. Don't say that..."* And a lot of these morals are from the Bible. Lying is one of them (Exodus 20:16).

*"So God is rewarding these women for lying? He blesses them with children after all!"*

The tragic reality about living in a world so broken by sin is that things aren't always black and white. It's not always easy to find out what is the right thing to do.

Fortunately, God has powerfully provided for us. Look at how Jesus prepares His followers for situations that may endanger their lives...

## SCRIPTURE

Luke 12:11–12

## READ

The Bible does give us very clear truths, things God does and doesn't approve of. And it's important for us to know His Word inside and out so that we may live the way He wants us to.

Alongside that, the Bible does not always give clear black-and-white answers to every *situation* we come across. This is one of the reasons why God has provided us with the Holy Spirit.

Once we receive the Holy Spirit, He walks with us every day of our lives. He provides wisdom on how to go about those not-so-clear situations of life. He coordinates conversations and prophetic moments with others. He uses Scripture to lead us in the right direction. He reminds us of His *character*.

The key is *engaging* the Holy Spirit throughout our day—not simply memorizing verses but speaking with Him, asking Him to provide us with clarity and insight. **Faithful living requires constant engagement with our very relational God.**

Oh how gloriously personal our God is! Not that He Himself is unique to each person, but that He walks with us where we are.

**The midwives were guided by what they *knew* of God's character to deceive Pharaoh. We are called to be guided by *the God living inside of us* to be faithful no matter the circumstance.**

## JOURNAL

**Pharaoh was afraid the growth of God's people would endanger his kingdom.** Sometimes we are afraid of God's ever-growing reign in our lives. As we walk with God, He asks us to surrender more of ourselves to Him. More territory, if you will. Are there areas in your life you are afraid to surrender to God? Are there any places you *don't* want Him to speak into? Are there any ways you are ignoring the voice of God trying to speak into those areas?

**The terrible circumstances of the Hebrews were outside of their control, but not outside of God's.** Perhaps you are in a tough circumstance now. Imagine if God made a prophecy about you going through this season like He did with the Hebrews. How would that change your perspective? How might it be encouraging? Empowering? How might it draw you closer to Him?

**The midwives were willing to risk their lives to save the children.** Is there anything God is asking you to risk right now for His children? A career? Relationship? Home? Lifestyle? Financial security? Dreams? What would need to change for you to risk those things for

His Kingdom? What is stopping you? Whose kingdom will you consider more important. Yours? Or His?

## CLOSING PRAYER

*"Lord, thank You that nothing is outside of Your control. You see where I am. May I be faithful no matter what. Please strengthen me. Help me walk by Your Spirit in all things. Amen."*

28

# Drawn Out

## OPENING PRAYER

*"Lord, please lead me today. May I trust what You want to do in my life today. From victories to setbacks, may my trust be in You and You alone. May I learn much about You and about how to live from this time together. I love You, my good Shepherd. Amen."*

## SCRIPTURE

Exodus 2:1–10
Hebrews 11:23

## THINK

- *Where is His grace?*
- *Where is His lordship?*
- *What do you think were the greatest difficulties Moses' parents had?*

## READ

We don't know the names of this Levite couple from Scripture, but they are listed among Enoch, Abraham, and David as remarkable examples of faith. Like the midwives, they refused to be afraid of Pharaoh and feared God instead. For three months, they hid their baby boy from the ongoing genocide. (Maybe you didn't realize that the murdering of the babies went on for so long.)

Hebrews 11 points out that they saw their child as *"beautiful."* He was worth risking everything for. They saw their baby the way God saw him: a blessing and beautiful image-bearer of their King.

Last chapter, I mentioned how five women will ironically be the ones to propel the future destruction of Pharaoh. Here we meet the other three: the baby's mother, the baby's sister, and the daughter of Pharaoh himself.

The baby's mother places him in a basket among the reeds of a river bank. Interestingly enough, the word used for "basket" here is the same word used for Noah's "ark." And both are sealed by pitch (tar) to keep from sinking. And both contain a faithful, imperfect deliverer that God uses mightily.

Now we can't know for sure if the baby's mother placed the basket in this spot intentionally so the princess would find him…but regardless, it is clear God is quietly orchestrating things in the background. The Egyptian princess takes pity on the Hebrew baby. And in an ironic reversal, she ends up *paying* the boy's mother to nurse the baby at the suggestion of the boy's sister.

It is the daughter of Pharaoh who also ironically names the baby Moses, which sounds like the word for "drawing out," because she drew him out of water.

Remember where we've seen water before? It's in the description of creation in chaos and darkness before God brings order. It's the chaos and darkness covering the earth during the flood before God "re-launches" creation.

In a way, Moses is the new Noah whom God will use to draw out His people from the chaos and darkness of slavery and into a "new creation": the Promised Land.

**Of course, Moses will become a foreshadowing of the even greater Deliverer who will draw out His people from the chaos and darkness of sin into a New Heaven and Earth...**

## SCRIPTURE

Matthew 2

## READ

In Jesus' time, it wasn't Egypt in charge, but Rome. Herod was an installed king over Israel on behalf of Caesar and Rome. So for him to hear about a *"king of the Jews"*...well, let's just say it might put him out of a job.

Herod might have been a more insane man than Pharaoh. History tells us that he even had some of his own family members killed out of paranoia. And here we see an interesting parallel between the magi and the midwives trying to protect innocent lives from these evil men.

In Exodus, God's people flee Egypt *to* the Promised Land. In Matthew, God's people (Mary, Joseph, and Jesus) will flee the Promised Land (Israel) *to* Egypt.

And did you catch *who* is actually looking for the King of the Jews to worship Him? It's not the chief priests and scribes (the Jews). It's the non-Jewish magi! This story in Matthew actually highlights the corruption of Israel during Jesus' time.

**Jesus enters history in a time of deep, spiritual darkness in order to draw out His people into the light.**

## JOURNAL

**There are a lot of ironic things that God orchestrates in this story.** Have you seen any moments of irony in your own life orchestrated by Him? Any hard situations you would like to see redeemed to bring Him glory? Like Moses, does your name have a meaning that highlights how He is going to work through you for His Kingdom?

**At this moment in the story, Moses is a small glimmer of hope during an incredibly dark time.** Perhaps you are going through a dark time right now. Perhaps the world around you feels especially dark. What glimmers of hope can you hold onto? Do you *have* hope? How can Christ provide hope? How have you seen Him provide hope before?

## CLOSING PRAYER

*"Father, thank You for drawing me out of the slavery of sin. Thank You for calling me out of the chaos and darkness of the world and into Your light and security. May I be a faithful testimony of Your goodness. May I be a vessel You use to draw out others. May Your Kingdom come. Amen."*

# 29

# Moses the Murderer

## OPENING PRAYER

*"Dear God, please make me more like Jesus. Living like You is the best way to live. May I learn more about how You live so that I may live that way as well. Amen."*

## SCRIPTURE

Exodus 2:11–15
Hebrews 11:24–26

## THINK

- *Where is His grace?*
- *Where is His lordship?*
- *Do you think Moses did the right thing? Why or why not?*

## READ

We are not certain how long Moses was nursed by his mother before moving in with the princess. Some think a few years, while others think it could have been until age ten or twelve. Either way, it appears that

Moses was aware of his Hebrew heritage, possibly from his faithful parents' teaching, before becoming incredibly educated and powerful in Egypt.

And what is the first thing we see this "new Noah" do?

He murders someone and hides the body.

It's reminiscent of Lamech killing a young man for merely striking him. It reminds us of Cain murdering Abel in a field where presumably his body would've been hidden from others.

From Pharaoh's reaction, it's clear that Moses didn't have governmental authority to do this. There's no command from God for him to deliver His people in this way or any prophetic moment where Moses knew he *was* to be the deliverer God used. In fact, God is very against us taking vengeance (Romans 12:19, Hebrews 10:30).

The fact that Moses *"looked this way and that"* before committing the act reveals his action was premeditated, not "in-the-moment self-defense." It's also what someone typically does before doing something they know is wrong.

Unlike Lamech and Cain, however, Moses seemed to be motivated by compassion. It emphasized that the beaten slave was *"one of his people."* Moses is trying to defend the oppressed, and he's assuming his people would have his back.

They don't.

This is the first of many moments to come where his own people push back at his leadership. But this first time, it's with good reason.

Like Lamech, Moses was trying to bring justice his own way. He was trying to be the *"ruler and judge"* over others instead of God. Later, Moses *will* be stepping into his people's interpersonal conflicts as a sort of ruler and judge, but God had not given Moses that role yet.

Despite Moses' sin, there is something admirable about his intentions and faith. He grew up in Pharaoh's palace and was raised to live like an Egyptian. He could have wealth, status, influence, popularity, power, and maybe even the throne if things fell his way, so long as Egypt was the kingdom and culture he was loyal to.

But instead, he chose to identify with God's people, the slaves! Hebrews 11:26 says he *"considered the reproach of Christ greater wealth than the treasures of Egypt, for he was looking to the reward."*

*"Wait...how could he know about Jesus?"*

Moses knew God was going to send a Messiah to defeat sin and save the world. Though his immaturity is on display here, his life was also directed towards obeying God. He valued God's rule in His life more than the government's. He valued God's culture instead of Egypt's culture.

## SCRIPTURE

Matthew 4:8–10

## READ

Just like Moses, Jesus had to choose who would really have the authority in His life. Would it be His Father and His Kingdom and Culture? Or Satan's? Satan offered Jesus everything just like Egypt did to Moses. And both decided that God's Kingdom was ultimately more valuable to them.

**Both Moses and Jesus thought the rewards in Heaven for faithfulness would be better than anything the current world and culture could give them.**

Moses did this imperfectly. Though he didn't want to build Egypt's kingdom, he tried to build God's Kingdom his own way, going so far as murdering someone to try to get it done. Moses had to be disciplined and humbled for God to use Him the way *He* wanted to.

But Jesus did this perfectly. Because of His faithfulness from start to finish, Jesus is on the throne in Heaven! And He will rule and judge earth completely in the future! But it meant He had to be disowned, betrayed, spat on, abused, lied about, beaten, and killed. That was the cost of forsaking Satan's kingdom and culture for His Father's.

## JOURNAL

**It is good to have a country and culture to be proud of and protect.** But does your love and loyalty to your country outweigh your loyalty to Jesus and His Kingdom? Would you give up your rights as a citizen to your country in order to honor God in all your decisions? When you see injustice in politics, do you bring your anxiety, fear, and outrage to God? Or do you spew out your feelings online to others? Do you ask God how you should respond? Or do you react in ways that seem right to you at the time? Do you think about how "history will see you" in this moment? Or how God sees you?

**There are some great things about your culture, and there are other things that dishonor God.** What are some aspects of your culture that highlight God's glory and character? What are some of the things about your culture that God disapproves of? What are ways you can specifically honor God's culture over those things?

**Moses had zeal for God and His people but went about obeying Him the wrong way.** When was a time you did something "for God" but later realized it was the wrong thing to do? How did you learn it was the wrong thing? Or perhaps there was something you believed firmly about God that needed to be corrected. How did God correct you?

## CLOSING PRAYER

*"Dear God, may I love Your Kingdom more than my country. May I honor You in how I view and go about politics. God, may my primary culture be Your culture of love, justice, forgiveness, and grace. And please help me disown the things of my culture that aren't glorifying to You. Amen!"*

# 30

# Moses at the Well

## OPENING PRAYER

*"Dear Lord, thank You again for this time we get together. You are so generous and good to me. Please help me be in wonder of who You are today. May who You are motivate me to be more like You. Please help and speak to me during this time. Amen."*

## SCRIPTURE

Exodus 2:15–22

## THINK

- *Where is His grace?*
- *Where is His lordship?*
- *What similarities and differences do you see between this story and the last one we looked at?*

## READ

Once again, Moses sees something unjust happening and steps in. But this time, it was in the right context and the right way. Not only that, but he goes the extra mile to take care of these women! Unlike Jacob trying to impress Rachel at the well, Moses acted because it was the right thing to do and he was able to do something about it.

In Egypt, he intercedes for the Jewish people the wrong way and has to flee the land. Ironically, here he intercedes for some Midianites the right way and is welcomed into their family.

Apparently, wells are the hot spots for relationships in the Bible. It's where Abraham's servant meets Rebekah and where Jacob meets Rachel. You could even arguably say that Adam met Eve by a "well" in the Garden of Eden because there was a river flowing out from the middle of it. Let's think about these well stories for a moment...

God brings Adam a wife because it was *"not good"* for him to be alone. God wanted Adam and Eve together to fulfill His promises to *"be fruitful and multiply."* After they sin, they hide from each other in shame and insecurity.

Isaac was mourning the death of his mother, and Rebekah was a source of comfort to him in that time. Isaac also needed Rebekah in order for God to fulfill His promises to Abraham to build a nation from him.

Jacob was on the run from Esau when he found Rachel and fell head over heels for her. He was looking for security, and he (unhealthily and at the expense of Leah) placed it on Rachel. Jacob also needed a wife in order for God to fulfill His promises.

Moses was also on the run but for murder and had lost everything. We'll learn soon that he became incredibly insecure about who he was as well. But God graciously provides Moses a support system and family in order to grow and, frankly, to stay alive.

In John, there's a Samaritan woman who visits a well, where she will meet the ultimate Love...

## SCRIPTURE

John 4:1–30; 39–42

## READ

Jesus was breaking several cultural taboos in this story. He was an unmarried man alone with a woman. He was a Jew and she was a Samaritan, whom Jews hated. Many believe that the fact she was getting water alone during the hottest part of the day reveals that she was an outcast from her people. Perhaps everyone knew her terrible history with men. But Jesus went out of His way to find her.

**This woman went to the well to fulfill a basic need in her life, but Jesus went to the well to fill her life.** He didn't come to the well in need. He *was* the well!

Here was a woman broken and insecure about her relational history, and she was met with the healing and secure love of Jesus. He purposely brought this pain up to her to prove how much He loved her. In a way, He's inviting her to be His bride! Her faith would make her part of the church after all.

This woman, who was trying to find love and safety in man after man, found the true river of life in Jesus. And Jesus wanted her to help fulfill His promise to spread the good news of His arrival to everyone around her. And she did! The whole town heard from her, and many believed in Jesus!

So often we are tempted to find love, security, redemption, hope, and life in relationships...boyfriends, girlfriends, spouses, parents, siblings, followers on our social media. And those can be great, amazing relationships.

But like Eve, Rebekah, Rachel, Zipporah, and the six men the Samaritan woman was with, they *will not* and *cannot* ultimately satisfy those very real needs. Maybe for periods of time, yes, but not in the long run and certainly not for eternity.

Jesus wants us to have eternal mindsets. He is the perfect "Husband," the perfect "Spouse," who *can* and *will* meet all of our needs, if not now then certainly in eternal paradise with Him.

## JOURNAL

**The Samaritan woman's relational history revealed a place in her that needed healing.** Are there any relationships right now where you are trying to find something in? Hope? Security? Value? Worth? There may be great, healthy things about the relationship(s) you listed. But how might Jesus fill those needs better? Are there any expectations you are placing on those relationships that should be found in Christ instead? Are the relationships you are pouring into stealing the opportunities from Jesus to meet those needs you want filled? Are they keeping you from really experiencing His unconditional, secure, safe, powerful, gracious, merciful, and life-giving love for you?

**Here we see Moses' passion for the vulnerable again, but this time it is in the right context and the right way.** Is there anyone vulnerable in your life right now that you can step up for? A kid bullied at school? A co-worker bullied at work? A client being taken advantage of? How can you step in appropriately? How can you go the extra mile for them expecting nothing in return? Ask God for wisdom and courage to do so.

## CLOSING PRAYER

*"Jesus, I want to want You more. I know I need You, but I do not even know all the ways I need You. I don't even understand how much I need You. But I know in my head I do. May I genuinely want You more. Please help me to put my faith in You rather than in the other 'wells' I try to find life from. I love You. Amen."*

# 31

# The Burning Bush

## OPENING PRAYER

*"Dear Father, You know me, and You love me. You know my weaknesses, my insecurities, my fears, and my anxieties. You know everything that is going on in my life right now. May I trust in Your love for me. May I trust in You. Please help me hear from You during this time. Amen."*

## SCRIPTURE

Exodus 3:1–4:17

## THINK

- *Where is His grace?*
- *Where is His lordship?*

## READ

Do you get the feeling that Moses isn't exactly stoked about God's plan? Here God was wanting Moses to be part of the greatest rescue plan in the world, and all Moses could think about was himself.

*"Who am I?"*

*"What if they ask me questions?"*

*"What if they don't believe me?"*

*"I can't speak well."*

*"Please send someone else..."*

Moses was dealing with some deep insecurities. Perhaps his brash attempt at saving the Hebrews his own way and failing worse than ever told him, *"You are a failure, Moses. Why even try?"*

Some wonder if Moses had a speech impediment that made him self-conscious. *"You're not good enough, Moses..."*

What we see in Moses here is incredible pride.

*"Pride?!"*

Yes, pride. Pride is making everything about yourself. Sometimes it comes across as humility, but in reality Moses is choosing his own way instead of God's way. He's thinking more about himself and his own shortcomings than God and His power. He's claiming that *his* self-perception is more important and truthful than *God's* perception of Him. Don't you see how arrogant that is?

If Moses was truly humble, he'd acknowledge his weaknesses but trust God in obedience. He'd say, *"I know I am incapable of doing this task without You, so please be with me as I say yes to You."* **Whenever we choose our own way out of fear or insecurity, we choose pride over humility.**

God addressed Moses' pushbacks in a unique way, but before we get to that, let's take a look at some things that Jesus said in Luke, things the disciples did in Acts, and things that Paul said in 2 Corinthians...

## SCRIPTURE

Luke 12:11–12
Acts 4:13
2 Corinthians 12:9–10

## READ

God tells Moses His name: Yahweh, which means "I AM WHO I AM." Anytime you see "LORD" in all caps in your Bible, it stands for this personal name of God. On one hand, He wants Moses to know that He is the end-all be-all God of the universe. And at the same time, He wants Moses to feel close to Him, to know Him as a friend and not just some distant spiritual being.

And then He wants Moses to focus on who *He is* instead of his own abilities or disabilities. He doesn't try to tell Moses, *"It's okay! You're good enough. You can do this!"* He wants Moses' eyes constantly focused on Him.

In Luke, Jesus encourages the disciples to rely on the Holy Spirit during the trials of their lives. There's no need for them to be anxious about the future because He will be with them.

Paul tells us in 2 Corinthians that our weaknesses actually give God room to do amazing things.

And the religious leaders in Acts 4 recognize that the only way Peter and John had courage was because they had spent time with Jesus.

Our personal inabilities give room for God to showcase Himself in our lives. He wants everyone to know how good and powerful and loving *He is,* and the best way for Him to do that is to use people who know they need Him.

Was Moses incredibly educated and competent? Clearly! But during those forty years of "exile" in the wilderness of Midian, Moses had been stripped of one kind of pride and now had to be rid of the self-ridiculing sort. Moses needed a different lens to see that it wasn't about him but about God.

God doesn't want people to be confused thinking, *"Well, Moses was extremely powerful or awesome or cool..."* No! He wants people following Him because He knows what's best for them. It's all about *Him*!

Now all this may sound arrogant of God, but it's actually quite humble of Him. He's acknowledging a truth about Himself and inviting us to partake in His goodness.

Think of it this way...imagine your life is a car and God is the engine. You need God in order for your life to work at all.

But imagine if the engine said, *"No, you don't need to pay attention to me. You don't need me to make your life work."* That'd make no sense! The car needs the engine just like we need God. God makes everything about Himself because everything *is* reliant on Him. That's not pride or arrogance. He's telling the truth so we can enjoy a fully running life!

## JOURNAL

**Moses wrestled with fear and insecurity at God's call.** Where are you feeling insecure, afraid, and/or anxious? What might be some ways that you are fixing your eyes on yourself rather than God? Knowing what we know about God and how He likes to work, what are some specific truths you can rest on to give you peace? What are some ways that God may want to display His glory in those situations?

**Despite Moses' insecurities, God had been preparing him to be a shepherd over His people by giving Moses the actual job of being a shepherd.** How have you seen God use your work/school/experience to prepare you for your current season of life? Any skills? Perspectives? Relationships? What are some things you are learning now that God may use in the future for His work?

**God has invited you to be a part of the greatest rescue plan in sharing the gospel with the world.** Look again at Moses' responses to God. Can you relate to any of those when it comes to sharing the gospel? For the ones you can connect with, how did God respond to Moses? How might God be responding to you? Will you obey?

## CLOSING PRAYER

*"Jesus, You are my true hope. You are my true peace. You are my true security. You want Your name to be glorified, and that is good news for me! May I rest in the goals You seek to accomplish in and around my life. May I obey like Moses ends up doing at the end of the day. I love You, Jesus. May my love of You grow. Amen!"*

# 32

# Bricks & Straw

## OPENING PRAYER

*"Dear Yahweh, thank You for being a personal God. You want me to get to know You, and You provide ways for me to do so. Thank You for Your Word that I may get to know You more. May I fall more in love with You, and may I honor You in all I do. Please bless this time together. Amen."*

## SCRIPTURE

Exodus 5

## THINK

• *Where is His grace?*
• *Where is His lordship?*
• *If you were one of the slaves in this story, how would you feel about the circumstance? About Moses? About God?*

## READ

Right before this story, Moses had a dramatic encounter with God. He had heard God speak with His own ears. He had seen miracles with the burning bush, the snake from his staff, and his leprous hand. God had promised that Egypt would see all His wonders and made bold claims that He would free the Hebrews from slavery...

And now everybody hates Moses.

Not only Pharaoh, but the Hebrews as well! Moses' obedience caused greater hardship on others. The very people he was trying to save (this time the correct way) rejected him once again.

This was exactly what Moses had feared in the first place. All of Moses' anxieties and insecurities were brought out into the open in front of everyone.

And just like any of us, Moses begins complaining to God about this. *"God, I told You this would happen, but You didn't listen to me!"*

Moses obeyed God and now his worst fears were happening. Empathy towards Moses is probably a good response from us. He's trying his best, he did the brave thing, and now things seem to be blowing up in his face.

It's okay for us to process our feelings with God like Moses did. He could have left altogether and forgotten the whole thing, but he didn't. Which is good because God was teaching Moses about Himself.

God had already told Moses that Pharaoh wouldn't listen to him. Perhaps Moses forgot that part or maybe he didn't want to believe it. God rarely promises things will go smoothly when we follow Him. If anything, He promises things will get worse.

In the below story, Jesus has already risen from the dead and told His disciples to spread the good news about Him. So here, His disciples Peter and John have just miraculously healed a man...

## SCRIPTURE

Acts 4:1–22

## READ

Peter and John's obedience to Jesus in preaching the gospel brought them before the religious elite. In other stories, Peter will be imprisoned for his faith, and we learn from church history that he will ultimately be executed for his faith. All because he was obeying God.

This is extremely important for us to understand: **Obeying God will not always bring immediate victory. It may make things worse.** It may increase your troubles, trials, and hardships. Like the disciples, it may bring imprisonment, beatings, and even death. You may lose friends, popularity, opportunities, relationships...following Jesus may even cause real suffering for others.

It's easy for us to expect things to go smoothly when we obey Jesus, but we need to drop those expectations. This doesn't mean we should become cynical and pessimistic. This is just being real about the world we live in.

Not only that, but God will oftentimes let things get a lot worse before He will act. Remember how long God waited before sending the flood and how long Joseph was in prison? Remember how much torment Jesus had to go through before He finally died on the cross?

It may be hard to hear, but this is who God is. This is how He works. **We may not like it, but our feelings don't decide what kind of God He is.**

But in these truths about Him we can find incredible peace. Knowing that obeying brings suffering makes suffering more bearable because we can expect it. If we understand that following Jesus will sometimes make things worse, then when the worse comes we can have greater strength.

Again, this doesn't mean we throw away our feelings or complaints. It simply means we let truth dictate our feelings and actions.

## JOURNAL

**Moses brought his complaints to God.** When you are suffering or going through a difficult time, how do you respond? Do you draw near to Him? Withdraw from Him? Spew accusations at Him? Pretend everything is okay?

**Moses obeyed God and it led to things getting worse.** When was a time you did the right thing and there were bad consequences? A time that led to difficulties for others? How did God speak to you during that time? Was there anything good that came from it? How willing are you to obey God even if it means suffering for others? (Remember, the resulting suffering *did* lead to blessing for the Hebrews later. God's heart is still to love others!)

**Moses accuses God of doing evil.** Have you ever done that? Is there anything that God calls good that you call evil? What are things that our culture calls evil that God calls good? Are there any things that God has done in your life that you thought were evil but later considered good?

## CLOSING PRAYER:

*"Lord Jesus, please strengthen me in this time. May I not be deluded to think that no trouble shall be brought my way. Instead, may my foundation in You grow only stronger, that I may glorify You in how I persevere when those days come. To You only be the glory. Amen.*

# 33

# The First Nine Plagues

## OPENING PRAYER

*"Dear God, sometimes You are confusing to understand. Your ways are not my ways. The way You do things doesn't always make sense to me, and I don't always like it. Today, would You help me learn more about You? Would You help me trust You more, especially with the things I don't understand? Amen!"*

## SCRIPTURE

Exodus 7–10

## THINK

- *Where is His grace?*
- *Where is His lordship?*
- *Why do you think God is doing things this way?*
- *Why do you think it was hard for Pharaoh to obey God?*
- *What do you notice about the nature of Moses' conversations with God here that are different from past chapters?*

## READ

Plague after plague, proof after proof, plea after plea...and Pharaoh would still not obey Yahweh. He didn't want to give up his power. He didn't want to admit that Yahweh was the true King. If you look closely, you'll notice that Pharaoh hardened his heart against God over and over again. Eventually, God continues to harden Pharaoh's heart Himself.

*"But why would God do that? Why wouldn't He just change Pharaoh's mind? Why all this suffering?"*

Like Adam and Eve, God is giving Pharaoh the dignity to choose Him. And if Pharaoh wanted to harden his own heart, God was patient enough to let him. Eventually, God helps Pharaoh accomplish his goal of rejecting Him.

It seems backward because of course God loved Pharaoh just like He loves any of us. He wanted Pharaoh to choose to be in a relationship with Him. Pharaoh could have chosen to follow Yahweh at any time, but instead he rejects God over and over again.

But in all of this, the people of Israel were protected. They were living in the land of Goshen within Egypt. Repeatedly these passages show that God was treating His people differently. Their experience of these plagues was very different from those who were under God's judgment.

Now today, when we ask to see God do miracles, we don't often mean plagues of judgment. We might even be thankful and think, *"Boy, I'm glad God doesn't do stuff like this anymore!"*

In some ways, that may be true. When terrible things happen in our world, it's not clear what may be God's judgment or what simply might be the result of living in a broken world. But what we do read in Scripture is a prophecy about what God is going to do in the future, and it may look a bit familiar...

## SCRIPTURE

Revelation 16

## READ

What we see here is a future series of events where God pours out similar plagues across the entire world. These things may happen in our lifetime, but no one is sure. But just like with Pharaoh and Egypt, God will send dangerous and terrorizing warnings to repent, and people won't. They will only harden their hearts against God.

*"Well that doesn't seem very nice! I don't think scaring people into following God is the right way to do things. Why is God doing things like this?"*

That's a great point! Christians are called to be representatives of God's mercy and gentleness. But we are also called to be honest about God's justice.

Think of it this way...there is a righteous King over a kingdom of peace. But His kingdom is filled with rebels who want to overthrow the King. They start ignoring the King's laws and call people to follow them instead. They begin to build small anti-kingdoms within the King's land. In order for the King to restore peace to His kingdom, He has to wipe out the smaller rebellious kingdoms.

So the King arrives first in peace. He tells people that He is good, just, and merciful. He calls them to abandon their mini-kingdoms and follow Him. But the mini-kingdoms have Him killed on a cross.

But the King conquers death and promises to return. He waits and sends ambassadors to peacefully call these rebellious kings and queens to give their allegiance back to Him. Some do, others don't, and others go so far as to have the ambassadors killed.

So the King will raise the stakes. He will bring plagues and wonders to display His power. He's begun His process of rightly re-taking what belongs to Him, gradually and by force. He was already patient, so He takes a different tactic. He proves to them that there is no way they can win.

Some wake up, realizing they've been foolish, and surrender to Him. But many others continue to harden their hearts. They won't lay aside their crowns. They refuse to have Him as their King. And so the King must remove them completely to establish peace and order.

This may sound incredibly scary, but it's important for us to remember a few things. First, if your faith is in Jesus, these plagues from God are not for you. You've already set aside your crown. Jesus has already taken the plagues for us.

Second, it should comfort us that God will bring justice. All these mini-kingdoms, even if they seem good, are ultimately bringing pain, suffering, and rebellion against the good that God wants to bring.

And third, these plagues and disasters are going to be temporary and the final torments before His followers enjoy eternal peace, rest, and joy with God!

## JOURNAL

**Talk to God about your feelings and thoughts about these passages.** I'd encourage you to do this out loud. Share with Him things you are thankful for, things that you're struggling with, things that bother you...and then spend some time in silence waiting for Him to speak. He may or may not, but it can be good to give Him the space to.

**The plagues God brings in Exodus highlights His power over specific Egyptian "gods" and beliefs.** I'd encourage you to do a quick search online to see the comparisons. In your context, God might be using your life to address certain "gods" of your culture. A call to be generous in a culture that values gaining as much wealth as possible. A call to surrender your rights in a culture that wants you to always fight for them. Are there any other "gods" or values of your culture that God wants to display His power and authority over?

**Pharaoh kept hardening his heart toward the commands of God.** Is there anything you have been hardening your heart about? Any commands you've been disobeying? Any anti-Biblical beliefs you have been holding on to? Any sins you refuse to confess? Take some time to humble yourself and let the Holy Spirit speak into those things. Refuse to be like Pharaoh and ask for His forgiveness, help, and mercy.

## CLOSING PRAYER

*"Jesus, would You help me trust in Your plan? May I trust Your sense of justice and Your sense of grace. Would You please call more people to Yourself so they don't have to experience Your judgment? Please save my friends and family who come to mind now. I love You. In Your name I pray, amen."*

# 34

# Passover

## OPENING PRAYER

*"Dear Lord, may I hear from You today. May I know YOU more. Not just more about You, but You Yourself. May the things I learn impact and inform how I live. May Your Word affect every aspect of who I am today. Teach me, my King. Amen!"*

## SCRIPTURE

Exodus 11–12

## THINK

- *Where is His grace?*
- *Where is His lordship?*

## READ

Pharaoh hardened his heart towards God's mercy. And God gave him what he wanted: a hardened heart separated from Himself. Pharaoh chose to put his kingship over God's Kingship.

And finally, God brings justice for what the prior Pharaoh did to the Hebrew baby boys all those years ago.

But even then, God is merciful! He gives everyone the opportunity to put their faith in Him. He had given the Egyptians 430 years to follow Him. He offered warnings in the form of the plagues. And here, He offered a lamb to take the place of the firstborn, whereas with Pharaoh there was no alternative.

In many ways, the blood on the door was a symbol of who was king of that household. Was it Pharaoh? Or was it Yahweh?

A lot of people struggle with passages like these because children are involved. It may seem harsh, but this is fair justice. God is not taking more than what Pharaoh took in the first place.

*"But what about the children??"*

The older Egyptian children also had the opportunity to put their faith in Yahweh. Perhaps some did! If they were to be struck down by God, it doesn't mean that they would not go to Heaven and be in eternal paradise with Him. But their parents would still deal with the consequences of their lack of faith.

*"Well, what about infants?"*

This is a good and fair question that a lot of people struggle with. The Bible doesn't say exactly what happens to infants when they die, but here are a few things we do know...

1) **All are born sinful, separated from God, and are deserving of Hell** (Romans 3:23; Romans 5:12; Psalm 51:5). This sadly includes infants. *"But they haven't done anything wrong!"*

We need to remember that sin is not first and foremost an action. Sin at its core is a condition we all have.

2) **God is just.** God knows they have limited capacity to understand repentance and the difference between right and wrong (1 Samuel 16:7; Jeremiah 20:12).

3) **We have one story that might give us some clues.** King David lost a child, and his response in 2 Samuel 12:23 is, *"I shall go to him, but he will not return to me."* This seems to imply that David believed he would be with his dead son again.

Though the Bible doesn't have a black-and-white answer to this question, I personally believe this is evidence that those who die in the womb or as infants are lovingly welcomed into Heaven by God. Either way, we can trust that whatever He decides to do with the life of an infant after death is just and fair.

Passover and the Exodus are two of the most important events to occur in Scripture. They will be referred back to over and over again.

1,500 years later, Jesus celebrated Passover with His disciples. But that night, its impact would change forever...

## SCRIPTURE

Luke 22:14–20

## READ

Jesus is both just and merciful. He is the "destroyer" of evil and the sacrificial lamb. What we learn here is that the Passover was always meant to be a foreshadowing of Jesus' true victory. After generations of slavery to sin, Jesus is going to destroy evil so the captives may be set free. But He is also the way out.

**In Exodus, God says a lamb can take the place of the firstborn. But God offers His firstborn son as the lamb to take the place of everyone.**

God took the heartbreak here. God poured out His wrath on His own Son that He loved. How painful that must have been! How hard it must have been to strike down His own Son so that we may live! Yet, He did it. And Jesus volunteered to take it.

His blood on the cross is more powerful than the blood on the door frame. And as we place our faith in Jesus by accepting this sacrifice, we declare that Yahweh is our King, that Jesus is our King...not Pharaoh, not Caesar, not the government, not our culture, and not ourselves.

And as God delivered the Hebrews of Egypt, He delivers us from the shackles of our sinful nature. We are no longer slaves to sin!

Not only that, but God has Israel plunder Egypt, like what a king does after conquering a nation. Between this and the plagues, Egypt has lost everything they had put their faith and hope in. Their land is ruined, their gods are humiliated, their children and hope for the future are dead, and their material goods are pillaged.

So it will be at the end for those who don't put their faith in Jesus. All else will fall before Him. And His people will receive abundance and eternal life in the promised land of the New Heaven and New Earth combined.

As God told the Hebrews to celebrate Passover in remembrance of His mercy, justice, and deliverance, so Jesus tells us to celebrate what He has done in what we call Communion.

## JOURNAL

**Communion is something that should be done regularly by Christians.** What is your attitude toward Communion? Do you treat it casually? Formally? Absentmindedly? Solemnly? Happily? How often do you take Communion? What do you tend to think about while taking Communion? Do you take time to remember what Christ has done for you?

**God gave the Hebrews lots of instructions regarding Passover.** Read over them again. Why do you think that is? What is significant about them? What is God trying to draw their attention to? Consider the bread and wine of Communion. Why did Jesus use bread and wine? Why does He want us to take it regularly?

### CLOSING PRAYER

*"Jesus, thank You for offering Yourself to take my place. Thank You for being a just and merciful God. Thank You for not forgetting about evil, but doing something about it. Thank You for giving me the chance to put my faith in You. Thank You for calling me to Yourself. May I glorify You more today. Amen!"*

# 35

# The Red Sea

## OPENING PRAYER

*"Dear Lord, may Your Word seep into every fiber of my being. May I live as You would have me live. Please help me focus during this time. May I walk away loving You more. Amen!"*

## SCRIPTURE

Exodus 13:17–14:31

## THINK

- *Where is His grace?*
- *Where is His lordship?*
- *How do you see God as King over His people?*

## READ

Look at the multiple things God is working to accomplish at once in this passage:

- He wants to lead His people in a way where they won't face war and turn back to Egypt.
- He's helping Moses fulfill a promise to Joseph 430+ years earlier (see Genesis 50:25).
- He wants Pharaoh to think the Hebrews are stuck.
- He hardens Pharaoh's heart to pursue the Hebrews.
- He wants the Egyptians to know He is Lord.
- He wants to wipe out Egypt's army and thus the threat to try to take the Hebrews back as slaves.
- He wants to execute justice on Pharaoh and the Egyptians for all their evil.
- He wants the Hebrews to be truly free.
- He wants the Hebrews to fear Him and trust Moses.

And there's probably so much more! Think of every story, every heart, every relationship, every unnamed person in this story...God is working in the lives of all these people uniquely and specifically as well.

It's this reality of God that should draw us to praising Him for His wisdom. We should praise Him because He is a master of making multiple things happen at the same time for His good plans.

Let this truth about who God is comfort you. In your life right now, God is working to accomplish multiple things on multiple fronts. He is working to:

- Shape you into being more like Him in the specific ways you need at this moment in your life.
- Bring people into your life that you may share the gospel with and/or be a light to in a way only you can.
- Bring relationships into your life that can be with you in your journey of following Him.
- Heal you in the areas there is hurt.

- Develop your gifts, talents, abilities, and passions with opportunities for things He wants to do with you in the future.

In all of these things, God tells the Hebrews to not be afraid, to stand firm, to be still, and to see how God is working.

Now obviously all of life is not meant to be lived waiting around for God to do things. We have parts to play. The Hebrews had to physically trust God by leaving Egypt and walking through the Red Sea.

God is urging our hearts to change toward courage, endurance, trust, peace, and anticipation of Him working in our lives. But this involves *action* in light of His trustworthiness, as Jesus tells us...

## SCRIPTURE

Luke 6:46–49

## READ

Jesus is calling us to trust Him both in our hearts and our actions. He is a sturdy rock, a strong foundation. The stories in the Old Testament specifically are meant to show us how we can trust Him with everything. These passages in Exodus show us that even in the unknown, we can trust that God is working things out for our good, as He promises in Romans 8:28.

The Hebrews did not yet understand this aspect of God: **that He will lead us into terrible circumstances on purpose to accomplish the good goals He has.** Jesus is telling us that trusting in Him implies we are putting His words into action.

God has given us every reason to trust Him. And maybe there are parts of your life where you still think, *"God, how could You let this happen to me? Why did you allow this? What possible good could come from this?"*

Maybe God will give you clarity on those things before you die or maybe you'll only understand the big picture afterward...but we are urged to take comfort in the fact that *there is* a big picture. It wasn't until the miraculous occurred that the Hebrews were able to understand what God was doing.

God's greatest gift was giving His Son for our lives. He is the God we can trust. And so Jesus shows us how to trust Him: by doing what He asks of us and letting the truths of who He is take root in our lives. This way, *when* the storms come, we can truly have courage, endurance, trust, peace, and anticipation of His deliverance.

## JOURNAL

**God did not want the Hebrews to go near the Philistines and experience war...yet.** They would later. But at this point, their hearts weren't ready, so God took them on a different route. What roadblocks are you facing in life right now? What dreams haven't happened yet? What are things you are hoping for that haven't occurred yet? Is it possible that God wants you to "avoid war" at this moment? That perhaps you aren't ready? That perhaps you aren't in a good place yet for Him to give you those things?

**The Hebrews were being led by a giant pillar of cloud by day and pillar of fire by night.** This was a blatantly obvious picture of God's presence and blessing. And yet they still feared for their lives and complained to Moses. What blatantly obvious things from God are you missing right now? What signs of God's presence have you forgotten?

What displays of His power have you let slip your mind? What promises of God have you disregarded?

**God did not miraculously build a bridge across the Red Sea.** He parted it—meaning the Hebrews had to walk through the sea trusting that God wasn't going to let the waves crash down on them. What might God be asking you to walk *through*? What trust does that require of you? In what ways will you have to rely on Him in order to get through?

## CLOSING PRAYER

*"Lord, would You grant me an eternal perspective? May I see things the way You see things. And may I trust You when I am unable to understand or see. You are a good God working to accomplish so much in and through me. May I rest in the fact that You will succeed. I love You. Amen."*

# 36

# The Songs of Moses & Miriam

## OPENING PRAYER

*"Dear God, it is sometimes hard for me to connect with You. Would You please help me connect with You today? May I hear Your voice. May I grow in the knowledge of who You are. And may this time shape me into becoming more like you. Amen!"*

## SCRIPTURE

Exodus 15:1–21

## THINK

• *Where is His grace?*
• *Where is His lordship?*
• *How are these two worship songs similar to songs you sing with the church on Sundays? How are they different?*

## READ

Godly men sing praise. Godly women sing praise.

The narrative pauses for a moment to highlight God's people worshiping Him. They can't help but sing!

The attention and focus is all on Him. They praise God for what He has done. For who He is. For what He will do. Moses and Miriam (Moses' sister who watched over him in the basket all those years ago) model for us the heart of worship.

This song in particular highlights God as a great warrior King. They call Him a *"man of war."* Obviously, God was not man (yet…). It's a metaphor to help us understand what they are getting at. He is the one who fought for them, rescued them, delivered them…almost like a knight in shining armor.

Music is a mysterious creation from God. At its simplest, it is merely a combination of sounds that sometimes includes words and instruments…yet music can pierce the heart.

Have you ever noticed how much music accompanies our lives? Important events like weddings, funerals, and graduations are made grander and more significant with music. Stadiums erupt in cheering songs when their teams score points. "Pump-up" music fuels our workouts. Christmas music brings an atmosphere of joy and community. Moving ballads help us process and express heartbreak.

God created music to touch our souls and help us express deep emotions and truths. Think about it…the first recorded words out of Adam's mouth were a love song/poem when he saw Eve!

This is one of the reasons why God calls us to sing worship songs together. He knows it moves our souls differently than just speaking. We remember songs easier than sentences. People singing together is a unifying experience.

Here, music is used as a joyful battle cry as the Hebrews begin to make their way to take the Promised Land. But sometimes it also articulates great difficulty...

## SCRIPTURE

Mark 14:22–31

## READ

Squeezed between the installation of Communion and the foretelling of Peter's denial is an intimate moment Jesus shares with His disciples. Before He leads them out to pray in the Garden of Gethsemane, He sings with them.

Most people think He was singing Psalm 113–118, called the Hallel, which means "praise" in Hebrew. (I'd recommend reading those psalms to dig deeper!) Jesus was singing right before the most painful experience of His life. It probably served as a comfort to Him and an encouraging proclamation of the goodness of God.

**If Jesus sang, we should too.**

Singing worship can have a variety of contexts. Here it was part of the formal ceremony that is Passover. In Exodus, it was the outpouring of what God had done. Throughout Psalms, you'll find worship songs meant for groups of people to sing together as well as more personal, intimate reflections.

If you are an artistic, musical person, you can probably already connect with the depth and wonder of worship through music. If that's you, I'd encourage you to read Exodus 15 again and let yourself emotionally connect with the poetry being sung. Put yourself in the shoes of the Hebrew people in light of what they just went through.

If you don't consider yourself an artistic, musical person and you don't find yourself connecting with the poetry here, that's okay. God has made us with a variety of different skills, talents, and bents. I *would* like to encourage you to not be passive in this area though.

Throughout Scripture, we are commanded to sing to the Lord (Colossians 3:16; Psalm 105:1–2). This means that even if you don't emotionally connect with what you are singing, it is still a powerful act of obedience to lift your voice in praise.

## JOURNAL

**Moses' and Miriam's songs directly related to the circumstances they just experienced.** How do you think this song affected their people? Are there any songs written by your local church that connect with something your community has gone through? What would the effect be if your church did have those songs? Have you written any songs/poetry about what God has done for you? (Try it!)

**The songs in Exodus portray God as a warrior King.** What are some of the pictures of God that are sung regularly in your context? Are there any patterns? How does this shape the culture of your church? How does it shape your perspective of God? Are there any pictures of God that are lacking or absent from your regular worship songs? If they were to be added, what might that do to the culture of your church? To your heart?

**Jesus sang.** Maybe He had a beautiful voice. Maybe He was tone-deaf. We don't know. But He sang. Are you comfortable singing worship songs? If not, how come? If you are comfortable singing non-worship songs, what do you think the difference is? What might be the next step to taking your singing worship "to the next level"? How might you bring more glory to God through singing?

## CLOSING PRAYER

*"Jesus, please help me remember all the ways that You have been there for me. Develop in me a true heart of worship through song. Help me grow in how I sing to You and for You. May I grow in connecting with You through worship. In the name of Jesus, amen!"*

# Daily Manna

## OPENING PRAYER

*"Dear Lord, thank You so much for this time together. I pray that You would open my eyes to see You more clearly today. I want to know and understand You more. Please teach me more about Yourself so that we can have a deeper and closer relationship. Amen."*

## SCRIPTURE

Exodus 15:22–17:7

## THINK

- *Where is His grace?*
- *Where is His lordship?*

## READ

The Hebrews have been delivered from slavery and are making their way toward the Promised Land (though they will make a pit stop along the way). Exodus 12:37 tells us the people consisted of about 600,000 *"men on foot, besides women and children."* So we can estimate anywhere between 1.5 to 2 million people along with *a lot* of livestock.

That's a lot of people to feed. And the "hangry" is setting in. The people start grumbling against Moses and then drag Aaron into it. (We haven't spent much time on Aaron, but he is Moses' older brother whom God sent to be a partner with him in this mission.) In Exodus 16:7, Moses tells the people they haven't been complaining against him and Aaron really; they've been complaining against God.

God has made it clear that *He* is the one who delivered them out of Egypt, not Moses. So when they think they are grumbling *against* Moses and how he's led them, what they are really doing is complaining *against* God and how *He's* led them.

He's the one who saved them. He knows the route He's taking them on. He knows about the lack of food and water along the way. If there's anyone they should bring their needs to, it should be God.

The hope is that if they do that, they would remember how faithful He had been already and choose trust in Him. Remember, God desires us to be honest and raw with Him. And He desires the intimacy that comes from such a relationship to drive us toward deeper trust in Him.

God does miraculously provide, but there is something going on in the background here. In Exodus 15:25 and 16:4, God makes it clear that He is testing His people.

We need to understand that He will test us at times. He'll use both big life circumstances as well as smaller day-to-day decisions as tests.

*"But doesn't God already know how faithful I am? Why would He go to the trouble of having me go through a test?"*

Think about taking tests at school. Tests aren't for teachers; they're for students. The purpose of test-taking is to display whether you have mastered the material or not. They are designed to expose you. You can also translate "test" here as "to prove by trial." Have you been listening? Have you been putting in the effort? Is what you're learning truly sinking in? Are you ready for the next stage? In a similar way, God tests us to see whether we have really "mastered" what He is trying to teach us.

When you fail tests, it exposes where you need to grow in your faith. It shows God's patience and grace with you. It reminds you of how much you need Him so that you will take steps to surrender to Him again.

When you pass tests, you get to celebrate how much you have grown and the amazing work that God has done in you!

Tests also serve as reminders. God commanded that some manna be stored as a reminder of God's faithfulness. God uses tests as measuring rods on our journey of faith to encourage us through difficulties.

## SCRIPTURE

Matthew 6:7–13

## READ

Jesus is teaching His disciples how to pray and uses this phrase: *"daily bread."* This is no doubt a callback to how He provided manna to the Hebrews nearly 1,500 years earlier.

Now Jesus isn't only talking about bread here or even food for that matter. He's talking about the things we need to get through the day, be it finances, strength, help, or whatever. There are two things we can see Jesus trying to do here.

The first is to fix our eyes on this "Giver of Bread." Just as the Hebrews were led through the wilderness to the Promised Land, we are being led by Christ to the New Heaven and New Earth. This was His idea, and He wants us to remain dependent on Him as sheep are dependent on a shepherd.

Why would Jesus want us to have this dependency? So we stay close to the Shepherd on our journey. It's not to make us feel bad or useless, but for our protection against the evil that would take us away from Him. Dependence on Jesus is for our good!

A second lesson we see Jesus teaching us is to keep our eyes on the immediate. Now there are passages in the Bible that speak to the wisdom of preparation and long-term thinking (Proverbs 21:5 and 24:27, for example). Alongside that wisdom, Jesus is drawing our eyes to **walking with Him** *today*. Not merely when things are tough, but when things are normal. **This awareness of daily receiving from Jesus builds in us gratitude, love, and joy in our relationship with Jesus that we couldn't have otherwise.**

*"But what about the times when He doesn't? What about the times Christians have starved to death or been killed by disease? Was God unfaithful?"*

These are very real and difficult questions. We need to remember that God has a perspective on our lives that we simply don't. As we have talked about before, He will use the evil and brokenness of the world for His good purposes.

Though no quick answer in this context can satisfy the emotional tug of a question like this, it is important for us to remember those big-picture truths of God's character. No tragedy is without purpose, especially for those who are currently in eternal joy with their Creator!

## JOURNAL

**Moses clarified that the Hebrews were complaining against God, not him.** Do you tend to bring your needs to God or to others? Yes, God may use others (parents, spouses, friends, churches, the government, organizations) to meet your needs, but do you *begin* by bringing your needs to Him? The nature of the Hebrews' complaints was accusatory of God's character. Are yours? Do you bring God your issues assaulting His character? Or do you bring God your issues *because* He is Lord and loves you?

**God was testing His people in the wilderness.** When was a time God tested your faith? It can be a big life-altering event or just a small interaction with someone. How did you do with that test? When was a test you passed? Failed? Are you in the middle of a test right now? What would passing this current test entail? What are some of the fruits that have come from passing tests in the past?

**Jesus desires for us to have a daily reliance on Him.** How has Jesus met your day-to-day needs on a regular basis? In unique instances? When was a tough season that You needed to rely on Him? A normal season? When was a good season You needed to rely on Him or *should have* relied on Him? Do you rely on Him when things are tough? Do you practice relying on Him when things are going well?

## CLOSING PRAYER

*"Jesus, You are my faithful Provider. You know all my needs before I can even articulate them. You know what I need even when I don't. Would You please help me trust You to meet my needs in the day-to-day moments? May I be faithful through all things You call me into. I love You, Lord. Amen."*

# Bearing the Burden

## OPENING PRAYER

*"Dear Lord, I pray that You would help me during this time. Please help me focus, concentrate, and really absorb Your Word in a way that I walk away changed. Please humble me and help me. Thank You!"*

## SCRIPTURE

Exodus 17:8–18:27

## THINK

- *Where is His grace?*
- *Where is His lordship?*
- *What impact is God's work having on the various peoples in this story?*

## READ

Meet the Amalekites, the first adversaries of the newly freed Hebrew people. Remember this nomadic tribe of people because they will keep showing up in the Old Testament. They are first introduced coming out of nowhere to take advantage of God's *"faint and weary"* people (Deuteronomy 25:17–18), likely trying to plunder the great wealth they gained from Egypt.

Fortunately, God miraculously provides them victory through Moses and his aide Joshua. He tells Moses to write this down *"as a memorial in a book and recite it in the ears of Joshua"* (Exodus 17:14). Joshua will need to remember this, and we will find out why in time.

We then get a story of Moses' father-in-law visiting Moses, hearing about what God has done, and then praising God. Notice how Jethro was a Midianite priest? Well, Midian was a son of Abraham's second wife, Keturah, whom he married after Sarah passed away (Genesis 25:1–2).

It's possible Jethro had also been following God all along, influenced as a descendant of Abraham. But I personally believe that he had been a pagan priest up to this point. Look again at how he responds to Moses' testimony in Exodus 18:11–12:

*"'Now I know that the Lord is greater than all gods, because in this affair they dealt arrogantly with the people.' And Jethro, Moses' father-in-law, brought a burnt offering and sacrifices to God..."*

We see how much Moses respected and honored Jethro, bowing down to him, kissing him, and asking how he had been doing. They had spent forty years together and were finally being reunited. And now Moses is sharing with his non-Hebrew father-in-law his testimony of what God has done.

Do you see God beginning to answer His promise to Abraham about blessing the world through this people? Jethro has put his faith in Yahweh from hearing Moses' testimony!

Jethro then proceeds to see how Moses is running things and offers him some fatherly advice: Get help.

Moses was the one who had seen God work countless times. The one who stood up to Pharaoh. The one whom God actually spoke to directly. **There was no one more mature in their faith at this time than Moses. And yet he needed others.**

Moses wasn't invincible. He was still human and dealt with physical, mental, and emotional limitations that come with being human. Even though he had the strongest faith, he literally was still not capable of carrying out every task. **Getting help from others was required for Moses' faithfulness, even though he was the most faithful person in the room.**

Maybe you've been following God for a while. Maybe you grew up in a Christian household and know all the stories, know the basics of following God, and have even seen miracles in your own life. Praise God if that's the case! But even so, if Moses needed others, so do you.

Our culture doesn't usually like the idea of getting help from others. It makes us feel weak, small, and helpless. Maybe you feel looked down upon when you ask for help. (Maybe you look down on others when *they* ask for help!)

But Moses learned and understood his limitations. It takes humility to do that. **Getting help from others is crucial for our spiritual health.** It's how God designed us. So when we refuse help from others, we are literally working against God's design.

## SCRIPTURE

Mark 14:32–50

## READ

Jesus was the most spiritually mature person in the room, and even *He* needed help. He was about to experience the most difficult thing imaginable: the very wrath and justice of God. And He was feeling incredibly anxious and alone. Jesus longed for support, encouragement, and prayers from His best friends, even though they couldn't possibly imagine what He was going through.

**Do you think you are stronger than Jesus?**

Jesus models how to be weak, vulnerable, and in need. He went to the Father with everything and placed all His hope in Him. And at the same time, He invited others to be with Him in what He was going through. Sadly, these friends weren't dependable. But even then, Jesus was humble enough to acknowledge He still needed them.

Now of course we should be wise with who we get help from. Some people may not always be looking out for our best interests. Others love us but don't point us to holiness and obedience to Jesus. But even then, God may use non-Christians to bring wisdom and guidance. (Jethro was a brand-new follower of Yahweh!) We should always weigh the wisdom given to us from others with the wisdom we receive from God in the Bible.

## JOURNAL

**After forty years of loving Jethro well, Moses shared his testimony of God's work, and Jethro put his faith in Yahweh.** Is there anyone like Jethro in your family? Someone who hasn't given their life to Jesus yet? How well have you been showing Christ's love to them? How consistent are you? Is it genuine like Moses' love for Jethro? Have you shared with them what God has been doing in your life lately?

**Moses needed help from Aaron and Hur to fight the Amalekites as well as from others to help take care of his people.** Does asking for help come easy to you? Why or why not? Are there certain areas of your life you refuse to get input on? (Relationships? Parenting? Your future?) What is it about those areas that cause you to close yourself off from help? What are some ways you can let yourself be helped by others?

**Part of our call as Christians is not only to get help from others, but to help others.** Who are some people in your life that could use your encouragement, support, and help? What are some ways you can do that?

## CLOSING PRAYER

*"Jesus, thank You for modeling weakness for me. Sometimes I feel like I need to do it all on my own, and You tell me that's not true. Would You please help me ask for help in all areas of my life? May I not be someone who is blind, stubborn, and hard of heart. May I be a humble follower of You, my Lord. Amen."*

# 39

## At Mount Sinai

## OPENING PRAYER

*"Jesus, thank You for this place and time together. You have been so faithful to me even when I am not. Please help me be more faithful to You today than I was yesterday. I love You, Lord. Amen!"*

## SCRIPTURE

Exodus 19:1–20:21

## THINK

- *Where is His grace?*
- *Where is His lordship?*

## READ

As God promised in Exodus 3:12, Moses returns to Mt. Sinai (Mt. Horeb) with the freed Hebrew people. But instead of a burning bush, we have a burning mountain! About fifty days after leaving Egypt, God's presence arrives in a pillar of fire atop the mountain. He covers it with cloud, smoke, thunder, and lighting and an increasingly loud trumpet blast as the ground shakes.

The people have spent three days cleaning their clothes and preparing themselves for God's arrival. (Note: The command to *"not go near a woman"* means to abstain from sex to prepare for this time.) God's call for them is to be a *"kingdom of priests and a holy nation."* **His desire for all of them as a nation is to be representatives of His goodness, justice, and love to a dark, broken world.** (Remember the third promise of the Abrahamic Covenant?)

The morning of the third day, when God arrives, will change the course of Israel's relationship with God forever. He speaks out the Ten Commandments for all His people to hear, setting the stage for the rest of the Law to follow. He then calls Moses up the mountain and begins the process of forming what we now call the **Mosaic Covenant**.

Like a marriage, God is committing Himself to Israel and Israel to Himself. **They alone are to be His people, and He alone is to be their God.** God will actually refer to Israel as His "wife" many times in the Bible as a picture to help us understand this covenant.

It's here that God gives the Law for His people to live by. Just like when a couple gets married, they adopt certain "laws" that shape their marriage. They commit to living together, sharing bank accounts, raising a family if they want one, not dating other people...Because of their status of marriage, this law affects every aspect of their lives for each other's benefit.

In a similar way, these laws are meant to show Israel how to be a good "spouse" to Yahweh. They will distinguish Israel from the rest of the world, show them what God cares about, and shape how Israel is run as a nation. And God will shower His love and blessings upon them.

We will talk more about these laws starting in the next chapter, but let's fast-forward a bit. Moses spends about forty days up on the mountain receiving the contents of the Law as the Israelites below start to get antsy...

## SCRIPTURE

Exodus 32

## READ

Yahweh and Israel have taken their wedding vows. But as God prepares how they will live life together, Israel begins to worship other gods. It'd be like someone having an affair during the reception on their wedding day.

God is rightly furious and heartbroken, especially after all He had done for them. And it is Moses who stands before Him pleading for mercy. Though all of Israel clearly deserves punishment for this, God relents and narrows His judgment to only 3,000, with the tribe of Levi stepping up to do the difficult task of slaying their own kinsmen.

The nation of Israel's start was characterized by God's wrath and mercy, but so was the Kingdom of God. Look at this dramatic comparison the author of Hebrews gives...

## SCRIPTURE

Hebrews 12:18–29

## READ

Every single person has "cheated" on God with idols just like the Israelites—not necessarily literal material idols but with other loves, passions, and commitments above Him. We have all chosen to reject His love for us at some point.

Moses pleaded with God for mercy, and God relented, narrowly pouring out the wrath His people deserved. **But Jesus was a better Moses. Instead of persuading the Father to relent, He offers Himself to be the *recipient* of the wrath for everyone.**

The author of Hebrews is pleading with Christians to surrender to Jesus in all things, not only because of how much better He is than Moses, but also because an even greater Sinai is coming. Mount Zion, the "heavenly Jerusalem," is the central city in the New Heaven and New Earth where God's covenant with His people will be made complete.

As followers of Jesus, we are living between Sinai and Zion, and we can rejoice at that! Everything else that is broken, corrupt, and evil will fall away. Unlike the Israelites, we are invited to approach the mountain of God (His presence) now because Jesus has interceded for us.

**Moses led Israel to Sinai to receive the Law. But Jesus leads us to Mount Zion to receive an eternity of joy, love, and adventure.**

## JOURNAL

**The Ten Commandments are the core of the Law highlighting God's heart for the kind of people He wants them to become.** His love and compassion brought them out of Egypt, and so in a sense, He says, *"I loved you this way first...now live with Me and each other like this..."* Going through each of the Ten Commandments again, how do they highlight His love for us? The kind of culture He wants to create? The kind of relationship He wants with His people?

**The covenant between God and Israel is like a marriage, as is Jesus' relationship with the church.** What is challenging about this picture describing our relationship with God? How might it affect our emotions toward God? Our actions with and for God? Our intentionality with God? Think of some godly marriages you know. What about them highlight the kind of relationship God desires with us? If you are married, how might your marriage more greatly reflect God's desire for us?

**Mt. Zion is the better Mt. Sinai.** Put yourself in the shoes of the Israelites at the bottom of Mt. Sinai...what might you be feeling or thinking? Now imagine approaching Mt. Zion with the description that Hebrews provides...what might you be feeling or thinking? What is encouraging about Mt. Zion being a *"kingdom that cannot be shaken"*? How can this truth affect your day-to-day life?

## CLOSING PRAYER

*"Jesus, thank You for leading me to Mount Zion. I want that Kingdom. I want to see the New Heaven and New Earth. I know I will because You have promised it. Please help me learn from the Israelites and trust in You in all things. May I love Your Word. And would You continue to speak to me today? Help me hear You. Amen."*

# 40

# The Law Part 1: Civil Laws

## OPENING PRAYER:

*"Lord, I love You. May this time be glorifying to You. May You do a good work in and through me today. May Your Word sink in and make me more like You. Help me, Lord. I love You. Amen."*

## READ

For the next three chapters, we are going to hone in on the Law. Leviticus and large portions of Exodus, Numbers, and Deuteronomy are all filled with the 613 individual laws that make up the Law of the Mosaic Covenant.

The laws of the covenant can be divided into three different categories: **Civil Laws, Ceremonial Laws,** and **Moral Laws.** These words aren't used in the Bible, nor will you find the laws organized this way. In fact, many of the laws will overlap in their categories. They are simply helpful tools we can use to understand how they work and what they're for. Today, we are going to look at some of the **Civil Laws.**

For the purposes of this study, we are going to take an aerial view of all three categories to get an idea of what God is doing here. But let's see what Jesus and Paul have to say about the Law first...

## SCRIPTURE

Matthew 5:17–20
Romans 3:9–20

## READ

In Romans, Paul explains that no one (except Jesus) has been able to follow the Law completely. And because of that, no one is righteous before God. But Jesus perfectly obeyed the Law in every way and so fulfilled its purpose.

Think about it this way. You are a student enrolled in school. And to graduate, you need to abide perfectly by certain "laws" of the school: go to class, take tests, follow dress code, etc.

Once you graduate having never broken one of these "laws," they don't apply any longer. You don't have to go to class, take tests, or follow dress code anymore. Those things serve their purpose while you are a student, but when you graduate, you are no longer under the law of the school.

Now imagine you break one (or more) of the rules so it becomes impossible for you to graduate. But then Jesus comes along. He is the perfect student, gets the diploma He deserves, and then turns to you and says, *"You want my diploma?"*

This is sort of how Jesus fulfilled the Law. And this is why followers of Jesus are no longer held accountable to it.

Now Paul clarifies in Romans that the Law provides *"knowledge of sin."* In other words, we can understand great aspects of God's heart and character through the Law. And that's what we are going to do here.

In this chapter, we are going to look at **Civil Laws.**

**Civil Laws deal with how Israel is to be run as a nation.** Remember, they've just lived as one big family under Egyptian rule for the past 400+ years. There's an estimated two million Israelites at Mt. Sinai, and they've never lived on their own before. Their influences are Egypt and the surrounding nations that certainly do not worship Yahweh.

**Civil Laws deal with crimes and how justice is to be carried out. It also includes ways that Israel is meant to be distinguished from the rest of the world as a sign that they belong to God.**

With our school metaphor in mind, these would be like the rules that could get you sent to the principal. *"Here's what happens when you bully someone...here's what happens when you are consistently late to class...here's what happens when you break dress code,"* etc.

Let's take a look at a few of them. Below, we will read one of these laws, get an idea of what it means, and see God's heart behind the law.

## SCRIPTURE

### Exodus 21:2

*"When you buy a Hebrew slave, he shall serve six years, and in the seventh he shall go out free, for nothing."*

In those days, if you were in a desperate financial situation, you could sell yourself as a slave to someone to pay off your debt. So in this context, the term slave is more like a servant (which is why the New International Version, or NIV, uses that word instead). God wants to prevent the Israelites from becoming like Egypt with its perpetual state of brutal slavery.

This law protects the rights of the indebted so they may not be taken advantage of. And it's patterned after the six days of creation (God working) and the seventh day that followed (God resting).

Here we can see the value God places on working hard. A capable person in debt isn't entitled to being taken care of by the government but must take responsibility and work to get out of it. And, at the same time, that work has a limit, highlighting God's desire for rest and relief from hard toil. It's a beautiful picture of God's heart for human dignity!

### Leviticus 24:21 and Exodus 21:15

*"Whoever kills an animal [that belongs to someone] must make restitution, but whoever kills a human being is to be put to death." (NIV)*

*"Whoever strikes his father or mother shall be put to death."*

Here we have two criminal justice laws about what to do when someone's animal is killed, when a human is killed, and when someone assaults their parents. We have the crime and the consequence spelled out so the government can carry out justice. Deuteronomy 19:15 makes it clear that there must be multiple witnesses before carrying out the death penalty, thereby establishing a legal due process.

We see that, according to God, human life is worth more than animal life. Animal murder only requires financial compensation, whereas human murder requires the death sentence. We also see how valuable God declares parents to be. God has a heart for a strong family unit that is characterized by love and respect.

## Deuteronomy 22:11

*"Do not wear clothes of wool and linen woven together." (NIV)*

Here we have a law that the Israelites must abide by as representatives of God's Kingdom. It is an outward expression that distinguishes the Israelites from the other nations.

It may be hard to understand the reasoning behind this one, but let's think back to our school example. Schools generally have a dress code that establishes and reinforces a certain culture of the school. Some private schools have strict dress codes to communicate a sort of "seriousness" about their education, attempting to limit distractions that various clothing may bring.

In a similar way, God is trying to get His people to think, *"Every aspect of my life is to be ruled and influenced by my love for God. Even my clothing."* God desires us to submit *all things* to Him for His glory.

## READ

The Civil Laws show us what God cares about, what He says is right and just, and the seriousness of our sin. They can teach us about justice. They can inform how we vote or create laws. You will see many laws about taking care of the widow, orphan, and immigrant in this category.

When Jesus came to proclaim the Kingdom of God, He wasn't putting into place a new system of government. There is no longer a national identity associated with being a follower of God. The purpose of the Civil Laws was fulfilled once Jesus came to begin the Kingdom of God, which is why Christians aren't meant to abide by these laws in their own lives. But we can still learn what God considers to be right and just from them and have them influence us.

## JOURNAL

**Understanding how we can grow in our relationship with Jesus from the Civil Laws can be tricky at times. But let's give it a shot!** Look at some of the Civil Laws below and see what you can learn about God. Think about what He cares about, His values, and what He desires for us, like we did in the examples above.

Deuteronomy 19:14

Deuteronomy 18:9–13

Deuteronomy 19:15–21

Exodus 21:33–34

Leviticus 11:1–12

## CLOSING PRAYER

*"Jesus, thank You for calling me into Your Kingdom. It is better than any possible kingdom or government made by mankind. May I honor You as Your citizen, and may I represent the Kingdom of God well. May I represent You well in all I do. Amen!"*

# 41

# The Law Part 2: Ceremonial Laws

## OPENING PRAYER

*"Father, may I know Your heart. May I know Your desire. May I know Your will. May I know You. I love You, Lord. Amen."*

## READ

The next category we are going to look at are **Ceremonial Laws**.

**Ceremonial Laws deal with how the Tabernacle is to be taken care of, how to be ritually clean and unclean, the roles of the priests, holidays, and the sacrificial system.**

We will spend time talking about the Tabernacle, priests, and the sacrificial system in more detail in a few chapters. For now, know that the Tabernacle was a tent that was set up as a meeting place with God, and the sacrificial system was used for making us right with God and was carried out by the priests.

Like the Civil Laws, Ceremonial Laws have also been fulfilled by Jesus, and therefore Christians are no longer bound to them. But let's be reminded by Jesus of the core calling of the Law...

## SCRIPTURE

Matthew 22:34–40

## READ

Love God with everything. Love others as if they are yourself.

That is the heart of the Law.

When it comes to the Ceremonial Laws, they focus more on how to have a deep relationship with God prior to Christ's sacrifice on the cross. They will serve as foreshadowings of what's to come.

Like last chapter, let's pull out some of these laws and see what we can learn about God's character and desire for us...

### *Leviticus 4:13–14*

*"If the whole congregation of Israel sins unintentionally and the thing is hidden from the eyes of the assembly, and they do any one of the things that by the Lord's commandments ought not to be done, and they realize their guilt, when the sin which they have committed becomes known, the assembly shall offer a bull from the herd for a sin offering and bring it in front of the tent of meeting."*

This law deals with how to handle unintentional sins the people commit. Remember that sins are crimes against God's Kingdom that require justice. The bull's death covers the crimes against God so that the people may be in a right relationship before Him.

We will go into more detail about the **sacrificial system** in a future chapter, but what we see here is God's desire to *be* in a right relationship with us. Even though we are so bad that we even sin unintentionally, God loves us so much that He is willing to set up a process for us to be good with Him again.

### Exodus 23:12

*"Six days you shall do your work, but on the seventh day you shall rest; that your ox and your donkey may have rest, and the son of your servant woman, and the alien, may be refreshed."*

This is one of the various laws concerning the **Sabbath**, which was a day of rest the Israelites were supposed to observe. Just as God rested from His work after six days of creation, they too were to abstain from work and rest on the seventh day of the week.

God displays His desire for not only His people to be refreshed, but animals, families, and immigrants as well. He cares that work animals not be abused by their masters. That the kids of servants get to spend time with their moms. That the immigrant with fewer rights not be taken advantage of. What a kind God!

### Deuteronomy 16:9–12

*"You shall count seven weeks. Begin to count the seven weeks from the time the sickle is first put to the standing grain. Then you shall keep the Feast of Weeks to the Lord your God with the tribute of a freewill offering from your hand, which you shall give as the Lord your God blesses you. And you shall rejoice before the Lord your God, you and your son and your*

*daughter, your male servant and your female servant, the Levite who is within your towns, the sojourner, the fatherless, and the widow who are among you, at the place that the Lord your God will choose, to make his name dwell there. You shall remember that you were a slave in Egypt; and you shall be careful to observe these statutes."*

Here we have a holiday called the **Feast of Weeks** that they were to celebrate fifty days after Passover. It will later be known by its Greek name "Penekostos," which today we call Pentecost. (You may know the incredible event that occurs during this holiday in Acts 2…)

As Abel brought the first of his flock to God, so God invites the Israelites to do the same with however much they want. As a "freewill offering," it's meant to reflect a heart of generosity in response to God's blessing over them. God's desire is for His people to be generous as He is generous.

And He desires rejoicing! Not just among the Israelite adults, but entire families and communities. Parents, kids, servants, co-workers, visitors, immigrants, orphans, widows… Imagine entire towns bonding and remembering God's goodness and provision over their lives! That's God's heart!

### Numbers 19:11–13

*"Whoever touches the dead body of any person shall be unclean seven days. He shall cleanse himself with the water on the third day and on the seventh day, and so be clean. But if he does not cleanse himself on the third day and on the seventh day, he will not become clean. Whoever touches a dead person, the body of anyone who has died, and does not cleanse himself, defiles the tabernacle of the Lord, and that person shall be cut off from Israel; because the water for impurity was not thrown on him, he shall be unclean. His uncleanness is still on him."*

When the Bible talks about being **clean and unclean**, it doesn't mean being good and bad. It typically refers to being ceremonially clean and ready for holy activities. This means that people who were designated "unclean" could not participate in holy things like offering a sacrifice.

It's sort of like when a fancy restaurant requires formal wear. Unless you have the right attire, you can't eat there. Or being on a sports team. If you want to get some time on the field, you need to be wearing your equipment. Otherwise, you are not ready to participate in the game.

In a similar way, these cleanliness laws were meant to be outward expressions of a prepared heart before God, as a wedding gown is an outward expression of a heart prepared to get married. God desires His people to be ready to engage with Him and what He is doing.

## READ

So what do followers of Jesus do with these laws now? Well, like we discussed with the Civil Laws, Jesus fulfilled them...

Christ was the final sacrifice to end the need for sacrifices to be made on our behalf (Hebrews 10:10).

In Christ, we are made clean and holy. We are now always able to participate in what God is doing and stand in His presence (Ephesians 5:25–27; Hebrews 10:22).

Holidays and festivals may still be celebrated, though they only celebrate the foreshadowings of what Jesus has done, like giving us an eternal Sabbath and pouring out *His* "freewill offering" of the Holy Spirit on Pentecost nearly 2,000 years later.

When we read these laws, we can be in awe and grateful for the ways God has poured out His love on us and connects with us now.

## JOURNAL

**Like the Civil Laws, it can be difficult at first to determine how Christians can be impacted by the Ceremonial Laws, but let's try!** Look at some of the Ceremonial Laws below and see what you can learn about God. Think about what He cares about, values, and desires for us, like we did in the examples above.

Leviticus 23:39–44

Leviticus 6:1–7

Leviticus 13:18–23

**Though we are not held accountable to the practices of the Ceremonial Law, spiritual practices can help us grow closer to Jesus.** What are some practices that may help you grow in your faith? If you have done any of these practices before, how have they impacted you? I recommend asking more mature Christians for things that have been helpful for them!

## CLOSING PRAYER

*"Jesus, thank You for Your Word. Thank You for these times together. Thank You that I am no longer under the Law but now get to do practices on my own to grow. Please help me grow my self-discipline and self-control for my own good and Your glory. Amen."*

# 42

# The Law Part 3: Moral Laws

## OPENING PRAYER

*"Dear Father, thank You for this time together. Please help me fix my eyes on You. So often I am tempted to make these times all about me. But I want my life to be all about You. Thank You for the ways You have been helping me do that so far. In Your name, Jesus, amen."*

## READ

Our final category is **Moral Laws. Moral Laws deal with how God's people are to conduct themselves toward each other. Think behavior, attitudes, relationships, and values.**

As with Civil and Ceremonial Laws, Jesus has fulfilled the Moral Laws as well. Even though we are not under the Moral Laws, we are still charged to be shaped by them. Let's go back to our school example to help us understand this...

When you graduate, you are no longer under the "law" of your school. So you are no longer accountable to the rules that deal with discipline because the principal is no longer your authority (Civil Laws).

You no longer have to adhere to dress code or participate in assemblies because it wouldn't make sense for you to do so anymore (Ceremonial Laws).

Many schools have expectations of behavior (Moral Laws). *Respect authority, be kind, be on time, be curious, etc.* These things describe what an ideal student looks like.

When you graduate, you no longer *have* to be an ideal student because you are not accountable to the school's code of culture. *But* these expectations were put in place to shape the kind of person you are to be *after* you graduate. You should *still* respect authority, be kind, be on time, be curious… And if you aren't, though the school won't punish you, you will naturally deal with the consequences of your actions.

**In a similar way, the Moral Laws paint a picture of the kind of people we are called to *become*.** Jesus uses the Law to prove God's heart in this in His "Sermon on the Mount" in Matthew 5. He takes a handful of these laws and reveals His heart about them. Take a look…

## SCRIPTURE

Matthew 5:21–48

## READ

The Law showed Israel how to live, but Jesus was trying to make it clear that sin is more of a heart issue than something to do with behavior. **In order to be a citizen of Israel, you needed to live under the Law. But the standard of living as a citizen of the Kingdom of God is so much higher!**

**Thankfully, Jesus met the standard for us. And now the Holy Spirit shapes us into becoming like Him so that the Law is *"written on our hearts"* (Hebrews 10:15–16).**

This is why we can learn so much from the Moral Laws. God has clarified what is right and wrong through the Law, and Jesus further clarifies His desires for us in the New Testament. **The more we know these laws and God's desire for us, the more we know the kind of God He is.** Take a look at some of these Moral Laws...

### Exodus 22:25

*"If you lend money to any of my people with you who is poor, you shall not be like a moneylender to him, and you shall not exact interest from him."*

God desires that the poor would not be taken advantage of. We are to lend in such a way that enables people to get out of their situations, not worsen it. Lending without interest is a sacrifice and risk. It reflects His generosity and the "risk" He takes of whether or not we will respond in a godly way to Him.

### Exodus 22:21

*"You shall not wrong a sojourner or oppress him, for you were sojourners in the land of Egypt."*

Just as God took care of them in their emigration to the Promised Land, He wants His people to take care of immigrants. He wants His people to value and not take advantage of them. God has a heart for *all* people.

## Exodus 23:4

*"If you meet your enemy's ox or his donkey going astray, you shall bring it back to him."*

God wants them to be the kind of people who look out for their enemies. We are natural enemies to Him, and yet He looks out for us. God desires a culture of community and togetherness, despite personal conflicts.

## Leviticus 18:22

*"You shall not lie with a male as with a woman; it is an abomination."*

God has a heart to provide a clear picture of His love for us. According to Him, it's impossible for any sexual relationship to do that other than a married husband and wife. He goes so far as to call the action an "abomination" because it profanes the very picture of love God has put forth. Husbands and wives reflect God differently in their respective roles, and so the combination of a man and woman within marriage is necessary for the picture of God to be clear (Ephesians 5:22–33). God desires to be clearly known!

## Exodus 22:22

*"You shall not mistreat any widow or fatherless child."*

God has a heart for the vulnerable. He intimately knows the unique struggles that widows, orphans, and the single-parented children faces. This pervasive law invites all His people to take care of them in whatever capacity they can.

## Exodus 23:2–3

*"You shall not fall in with the many to do evil, nor shall you bear witness in a lawsuit, siding with the many, so as to pervert justice, nor shall you be partial to a poor man in his lawsuit."*

God values standing "against the grain" if it is the right thing to do. He values courage, conviction, and integrity. He values justice that is carried out properly and fully.

And alongside His heart for the poor and marginalized, He wants His people to be careful to not act unjustly in their favor. One's circumstance may require compassion, but it would be wrong to grant them unjust favor simply because of their circumstance.

## JOURNAL

**As we did with the Civil and Ceremonial Laws, let's practice discovering God's heart behind some of the Moral Laws.** Think about the kind of people God wants them to become and how it reflects His love, values, and justice.

Leviticus 18:18

Leviticus 19:9–10

Leviticus 19:17–18

Leviticus 19:31

Leviticus 19:32

## CLOSING PRAYER

*"Jesus, You have a beautiful heart. I don't even understand the fullest depths of it. Your motivations are always pure, and You desire me to be just like You. Please continue to teach me what You are like so I may be like You. I love You, Lord. Amen."*

43 |

# The Tabernacle

## OPENING PRAYER

*"Lord, thank You for this place to meet with You now. May I hear from You. May I be changed by You. May I know You more, my good Jesus. To You be the glory in this time. Amen."*

## SCRIPTURE

Exodus 25:1–9
Exodus 31:1–11
Exodus 40:34–38

## THINK

- *Where is His grace?*
- *Where is His lordship?*
- *What details given seem most significant to you?*

## READ

In chapters 25 through 31, God gives Moses the designs for the **Tabernacle**, sometimes referred to as the **Tent of Meeting**. This is an astounding declaration because it means that God's presence will be dwelling among His people. Do you remember the last time that happened?

Eden.

The Israelites are beholding God's glory atop Mt. Sinai, and now God declares that He's coming down to be with them.

Right off the bat, God invites His people into what He's doing by asking them to give whatever they feel moved to give to make this project happen. Does God *need* them to do this? Couldn't He just have built the Tabernacle Himself? Sure, but that's not how He does things. He wants His people involved in the process.

And, in a way, we see God's mind at work as He prepares to create, drawing us back to Genesis 1 once again. His level of detail, craftsmanship, and intentionality are beautifully highlighted here.

Only this time, it will be His people creating for Him. He chooses two skilled craftsmen named Bezalel and Oholiab. But did you notice who also shows up to create?

The Holy Spirit.

The last time we saw Him mentioned, it was in Genesis 1:2. And what was He about to do?

Create.

More specifically, He was about to create a place where God would live among people. And He's about to do it again, this time through Bezalel. Chapters 35 through 40 of Exodus show us the follow-through of this construction.

For the purposes of this study, we won't be going into all of the details of the Tabernacle and its furnishings, but I *highly recommend* researching pictures and videos of the Tabernacle online so you can get a visual idea of what it generally looked like. I also *highly recommend* doing a little research on each of the items used in the Tabernacle and the symbolism behind their functions.

Remember, God gave us all of these details for a reason. They *will* point us back to Him and reveal His beauty to us if we give Him the time and mental effort to show us. (I've provided a list to get you started in the Journal section at the end of this chapter.)

What I *will* highlight is the **Holy of Holies**, which is located in the furthest-back portion of the tent. In it was the **Ark of the Covenant**, and atop that was an empty space called the **Mercy Seat** with two cherubim statues on either side.

In this space, God's presence would descend in a pillar of cloud or fire to metaphorically sit upon the Mercy Seat and use it as a throne. It's as if God is getting off His throne in Heaven, where He is surrounded by a heavenly host of spiritual beings, and coming to sit down on this "miniature throne" beside two statues of spiritual beings (Exodus 25:21–22; Revelation 4:3–8).

This is incredible! God is coming to dwell with His people! But then we see a detail that breaks our hearts...

## SCRIPTURE

Exodus 26:30–35

## READ

A veil prevents God's people from entering the place of His presence. And woven into the fabric of this curtain wall are images of cherubim. What does this remind us of?

It's the cherubim that guard the way into the Garden of Eden, preventing Adam and Eve from ever entering again.

We are reminded of our sin. That we are unable to stand in His presence. And though God has done something incredible and awe-inspiring, we are still not able to truly be *with* Him.

That is, until Jesus works. (Note that in the story below, "the Temple" mentioned has replaced the Tabernacle but maintains the same structural symbolism.)

## SCRIPTURE

Luke 23:44–49

## READ

On the night of Passover, the holiday remembering God's deliverance of Israel from slavery, Jesus is chosen as the unblemished lamb to be sacrificed. And the following day, He is killed. What happens as that is happening?

The curtain is torn in two.

The cherubim have been removed. The "flaming sword" has been sent away. The way to re-enter God's presence has been opened.

But just like in Exodus, *God* is the one who comes toward us yet again...

## SCRIPTURE

Acts 2:1–4

## READ

Fifty days after the first Passover, God's presence came upon Mt. Sinai in cloud, smoke, thunder, and lightning. Fifty days after the Passover when Jesus was offered up, God's presence came again accompanied by a mighty, rushing wind.

Except this time, it was not in one giant pillar of fire upon a mountain, but in small tongues of fire upon individuals. **God's people themselves become the new Tabernacle where He dwells.**

## JOURNAL

**God's heart has always been to dwell with us.** Does your heart *desire* to dwell with Him? Do you enjoy spending time with Him? Do you delight in His Word? Do you eagerly await the next time you can be alone with Him? Do you rejoice seeing *Him* abide in the believers you know? If you find yourself lacking in these desires, ask Him to give them to you!

**The first person in Scripture we see specifically filled with the Holy Spirit was the craftsman Bezalel.** Jesus was likely a craftsman too because of His earthly dad's profession (Matthew 13:55). List out the ways He empowered Bezalel to do the work he was called to do. In what ways have you seen God's empowerment in *your* work? What skills has God developed in you? How might you do your work *with* the Holy

Spirit to build an "Eden" in your context? Like the contributions toward the Tabernacle, what work might God be calling *you* to contribute to financially?

**I highly recommend taking time to read through the details of the main Tabernacle furnishings below to see what else you can discover about God's character:**

- The Ark of the Covenant – Exodus 25:10–22
- The Table for Bread – Exodus 25:23–30
- The Golden Lampstand – Exodus 25:31–40
- The Tabernacle – Exodus 26
- The Bronze Altar – Exodus 27:1–8
- The Court of the Tabernacle – Exodus 27:9–19
- The Altar of Incense – Exodus 30:1–10
- The Bronze Basin – Exodus 30:17–21

## CLOSING PRAYER

*"Lord, Your love for me is astounding, that You would fill me with Your very presence. May I desire You exponentially more than I do now, as You desire me. Create in me a heart that sincerely loves every word You have given me in Scripture, that I might further delight in You. I love You, Lord. Amen."*

## 44

# The Priests & the Levites

## OPENING PRAYER

*"Lord, thank You for calling me to You. May I honor You well. May I glorify You well. May I be more greatly prepared for Your Work as a result of this time together. Amen."*

## READ

Quick note here: It may be helpful to read the following chapter in a translation like the NLT, as some of the language may be more difficult to understand at first.

## SCRIPTURE

Numbers 18

## THINK

- *Where is His grace?*
- *Where is His lordship?*
- *How would you explain the role of the priests to someone who's never read this before?*

## READ

God establishes the Tabernacle as a place to meet with His people. But as we learned, the people cannot enter His presence because of their sin. They will need a mediator to stand between and purify them. This is where the **priests** come in.

God selects Aaron to be the **High Priest** over them, with his sons and future descendants serving as a priestly lineage. In order to serve, they must go through a variety of rituals to purify themselves since they themselves are sinful. They will be the ones to carry out **the sacrificial system** and other holy duties, which we will look at in the next chapter.

Now, a whole nation is a lot of people to serve, so they will need help. So God chooses the Levite tribe to be the chosen helpers of the priests. (As a reminder, a Levite is a descendant of Jacob's son Levi.)

The Levites were called to assist the priests with their work and look after the Tabernacle. They would live off the tithes (that is, 10% of the people's income) and portions of the sacrifices brought by the people. It's similar to how your local church likely meets the needs of your pastor through monthly giving.

God wanted the whole nation to be representative of His character (Exodus 19:6), but it was only the priests who could reconcile people to God at that time.

That all changed with Jesus.

But Jesus wasn't a descendant of Aaron. He was from the tribe of Judah, the fourth son of Jacob. How could He rightfully be a priest? Fortunately, the Bible shows us how from a strange story about Abraham and a mysterious visitor...

## SCRIPTURE

Genesis 14:18–20

Hebrews 7

## READ

Who the heck was Melchizedek?! We have no genealogy on him or record of his *"beginning of days nor end of life."* We know he's from Salem (possibly Jerusalem, which would later be the capital of Israel). But it appears he is simply an ordinary man whom God made a priest. Abraham even gives him a tenth (aka tithe) as an offering.

The point that Hebrews makes is that God is the one who picks His priests. Yes, He appointed the priesthood of Aaron's line, but He also chose Melchizedek. Therefore, God can choose Jesus to be an even greater priest. **Aaron and his descendants would die, but Jesus serves as an eternal priest with an authority established forever to connect us with the Father.**

When the Law was fulfilled, the duty of Aaron's line was fulfilled as well. **The Israelites under the Mosaic Covenant needed priests to connect us with God, but under the new covenant with Jesus, we** *all* **become priests...**

## SCRIPTURE

1 Peter 2:4–10

## READ

**Jesus became the ultimate High Priest mediating for us. And now** *we the church* **are the priests serving under Him.**

On earth, we serve on behalf of our High Priest reconciling people to God. And we have *even greater* power than the priests in Aaron's day because the Holy Spirit resides not in a Tabernacle, but in us! What beautiful work and power we have!

## JOURNAL

**We *all* are priests of God's Kingdom.** Pastors and elders are not the "new priests," church staff are not the "new Levites," and the congregation is not the "new Israel." *Every single Christian is a priest. There is no distinction.* How does this reality change your sense of responsibility to share the gospel? How you participate in your local church? How you live your life? How you see your life?

**God declares us to be *royal* priests.** How? Because we are also adopted by God, brother to King Jesus (Ephesians 1:5). How might that inform how you serve as a priest in your community? How you share the gospel? How you love others? How you disciple others to step into their "royal priesthood" themselves?

**Because of Jesus' High Priesthood, we have constant direct access to God.** How can this truth affect the way you pray? What you pray for? How you pray? When you pray? How can this influence your prayers for others when you are with them? When you are not with them?

## CLOSING PRAYER

*"Jesus, may I not grow weary in prayer. May I not grow weary in bearing witness about Your gospel. May I not grow weary in representing You. Please, my High Priest, may I be faithful unto You. Amen."*

# 45

# The Day of Atonement

## OPENING PRAYER

*"Lord, may You be praised during this time. May You be made much of. May my imagination be captured by Your Word today that I may follow You in greater wholeheartedness. Teach me Your ways, O Lord. I love You. Amen."*

## READ

The first five books of the Bible are called the Pentateuch, and it is widely held that they were largely authored by Moses. And Leviticus 16 is at the literal center of it. It will be the crux of the entire Pentateuch and the ultimate foreshadowing of Christ pouring out His love on us.

Like last chapter, it may be helpful to read the following Scripture in the New Living Translation first for clarity's sake.

## SCRIPTURE

Leviticus 16

## THINK

- *Where is His grace?*
- *Where is His lordship?*
- *How might you feel if you were Aaron during this process? If you were an Israelite witnessing it?*

## READ

Sacrifices and offerings were primary ways the Israelites were to express their hearts to God. Some were made as an act of worship and gratitude toward God; others were done to deal with sin.

God desired a relationship with His people. But He could not let their sins go unpunished. A payment would have to be made. Just like if you were to break the law today, the government would execute justice by making you pay a fine or spend time in prison. So God established the **sacrificial system** to process those payments.

Without going into all the details that Exodus through Deuteronomy provide, a person would recognize their guilt and bring a specific animal to the priests at the Tabernacle who would then carry out the sacrifice according to the statutes in the Law.

The most significant sacrifice of all was made on the **Day of Atonement**, sometimes called **Yom Kippur**.

Once a year, the High Priest was to purify himself in a variety of rituals and offer a bull to cover the sins of him and his family. He then would take two goats. He would confess the sins of all the people on one, the "scapegoat," and cast it out into the wilderness as it symbolically takes the sins away from the people. The people would then be in right standing with God.

The other goat was sacrificed, dying in the place of the Israelites. Its blood would then be sprinkled on the Mercy Seat atop the Ark of the Covenant. And God in His great mercy and love would accept the sacrifice.

This process was to happen once every year. And certainly thousands upon thousands of other sacrifices would have to be made throughout the year. Even though God had graciously offered this as a path to right standing with Him, what does this whole process of repeatedly offering sacrifices to pay for sins imply?

That no animal sacrifice could truly take away sins (Hebrews 10:4).

Something else would have to be done. And what we learn is that God laid out the Tabernacle, the priesthood, and the sacrificial system incredibly specifically for a reason...

## SCRIPTURE

Hebrews 8:1 –6
Hebrews 9:11–14
Hebrews 10:1–18

## READ

What we learn from that first passage is that the Tabernacle is an "earth version" of Heaven, a copy and foreshadowing of what is to come. That's a reason why God's instructions were so specific in its design. It's an earthly "mock-up" of God's throne room.

And it's why we needed Jesus. We needed a High Priest who could enter into Heaven's "holy of holies."

Jesus was the scapegoat, who bore our sins and cast them out *"as far as the east is from the west"* (Psalm 103:12).

He was the goat that was slain to pay the penalty for our sins, His pure blood greater and more significant than that of an animal's.

But it wasn't enough for Jesus to just *die* for our sins. He also needed to rise from the dead. Why? Because none of us are pure enough to carry His blood into the throne room of Heaven itself.

Because Jesus rose from the dead and ascended to Heaven, He was able to enter that "holy of holies." And as the High Priest, He presented His own blood on Heaven's Mercy Seat to pay for our sins.

Now, we are part of something greater than the Mosaic Covenant. It's the new covenant of Jesus Christ, where sacrifices are no longer required and we are forever forgiven!

## JOURNAL

**Under the old covenant, God's people would need to offer sacrifices for their sins continually, while we don't under the new covenant.** Imagine being under the old covenant and compare it with being under the new one. How might your perspective of God differ? Of sin? Of forgiveness? Of grace? Of obedience to God? Of fear? Of joy?

**Hebrews 10:6 says,** *"in burnt offerings and sin offerings You have taken no pleasure."* Though God was the one who put the sacrificial system into place, why do you think He didn't take pleasure in it? What might be some "problems" with the sacrificial system? What about it might break His heart? Upset Him?

**Understanding the details of the old covenant helps us understand what Christ did for us.** Take some time to reflect. How have these past several chapters on the Law, Tabernacle, priesthood, and sacrificial system affected Your picture of God? Your understanding of what Christ did for us? Your ability to enjoy seemingly "drier" parts of Scripture?

## CLOSING PRAYER

*"Lord, You are a purposeful God. All things have been done in Your great wisdom and love. Thank You for granting me the privilege of knowing Your Word and what You have done for me. I love You, Lord. Amen."*

# 46

# Refusing the Promised Land

## OPENING PRAYER

*"Lord, may I be deeply impacted by Your Word today. Please speak to me clearly, boldly, and tenderly. May I receive Your word humbly and ready to obey. I love You, Lord Jesus. May You be glorified in this time. Amen."*

## READ

The events at Mt. Sinai have finished. The Hebrew people have been given the Law, becoming the nation of Israel and fulfilling God's first promise to Abraham.

The stage has been set. Israel is to be a kingdom of priests to serve as a beacon of light to a dark world. Their mission is to love and obey God in everything as His representatives. It is now time for God to lead them to the land He's promised to give them: Canaan.

## SCRIPTURE

Numbers 13–14

## THINK

> • *Where is His grace?*
> • *Where is His lordship?*
> • *Make a list of all the ways Israel has seen God at work since Moses' mission began.*

## READ

Despite all God had done, the Israelites chose fear. After returning from their forty-day mission, ten of the twelve spies terrify the people, warning of incredibly fortified cities and giants. They even claim the Anakites to be Nephilim (though they had long since perished in the flood). And now the Israelites want to abandon the covenant, the call, and the mission and return to Egypt.

In Numbers 14:22, God declares His fury that these people have challenged His character ten times up until this point. (See if you can identify them!) Who else challenged God's character ten times?

Pharaoh.

Israel is behaving like Pharaoh, ignoring God's signs and wonders. They desire the kingdom of Egypt rather than God's Kingdom. They prefer the comfort of slavery, which they know, rather than the unknown blessings God intends for them to have. If only they had courage.

Back in Exodus 34:6–7, God gave Moses a description of Himself. In Numbers 14:17–18, Moses quotes His words back to Him, seemingly persuading God to not destroy the Israelites altogether. (Exodus 34:6–7 will actually be the most re-quoted verse within Scripture.)

As a consequence, the Israelites will not be allowed to take the land until all the fighting-aged men (ages twenty and older) who grumbled against the Lord have died. Because of their fear and distrust, the entire people will wander in the wilderness for forty years.

Only two of those men will be able to enter. Joshua, whom we met earlier, is one of them. His name used to be Hoshea, which means "he saves," but Moses renamed him Joshua which means "Yahweh saves." Apparently, he took that to heart.

The other is Caleb from the tribe of Judah, the same tribe Jesus descended from.

## SCRIPTURE

Matthew 15:32–16:12

## READ

Jesus feeds 4,000 men in this story, besides women and children, meaning there could've been thousands more there. The disciples had seen Him do this before, feeding over 5,000 that first time (Matthew 14:13–21).

Though the Pharisees and Sadducees may not have seen these exact miracles in person, they were certainly aware of the signs and wonders Jesus had been doing. Yet they still ask for a sign. Their hearts are refusing to believe that Jesus is who He says He is.

In Numbers, the spies were hardened against God's charge to take the land due to their fear. So were the Pharisees. What would happen to them if they were to lose their power, their influence, their sense of control, and the way they saw reality?

It was their fear and resulting pride that drove the Pharisees to crucify Christ. And it was the fear of the few spies that drove the masses away from trusting God and toward disobedience.

And so Jesus warns the disciples of the Pharisees' teaching, describing it as leaven. If they're not careful, it will infiltrate their hearts and minds. In a sense, Jesus is calling them to be like Caleb and Joshua.

## JOURNAL

**There are many voices in our day-to-day that try to drive us toward ungodly fear.** What are some of those voices? Why might they fearmonger? What might be driving *their* fear? Does their fear drive you to be like the masses or like Caleb and Joshua? Do you find yourself fearing what they fear? What steps might you take to prevent the "leaven" of their voices from infiltrating your life? How can you redirect your ungodly fear in godly fear?

**Though God says the next generation will inherit the Promised Land, they *will* suffer due to their parents' lack of faith.** Where are you lacking faith currently? How serious do you take your lack of faith in that area? How might your fear and lack of faith cause your kids to suffer? (If you are not a parent, you certainly still have an influence on the next generation of Christians!) How might it affect other believers? (Caleb and Joshua had to wander too!) How might it affect the culture at large? (The women and children had to live with the consequences of the men's actions!) With this in mind, what steps can you take to *choose* faith and *choose* courage? Pray and ask the Lord for help on this!

**Despite God's words, the fighting men try to backtrack and undo the consequences of their actions, but it leads to disaster.**

Initial cowardice and lack of faith prevented them from receiving God's blessings. God is gracious and will still do good with our cowardice (Romans 8:28), but it doesn't mean we haven't missed opportunities to receive His blessing. What blessings might you have missed in the past? What blessings might you be missing now? Do you take the blessings from faithfulness seriously? Are you ruthless at trying to expel sin from your life so that you can better experience His goodness?

## CLOSING PRAYER

*"Jesus, You displayed perfect courage when You climbed that hill to Calvary. May I do the same. May ungodly fear and the leaven of the fearful have no hold on me. Make me into a fortress for Your Kingdom's sake. Help me, my good Lord. Amen."*

# 47

# The Disqualification of Moses

## OPENING PRAYER

*"Lord, thank You for this time. May I receive what You have for me to-day. May I become more like You, glorifying You in all things. May Your name be made great in me and through me. Amen."*

## SCRIPTURE

Numbers 20:2–13

## THINK

- *Where is His grace?*
- *Where is His lordship?*
- *What do you make of the people accusing God and Moses over and over again despite God's past work?*

## READ

After all that, Moses would not be allowed to enter the Promised Land. How could this happen?!

The Israelites were attacking God's character and His chosen leader once again. And, once again, God mercifully provides a way to meet their needs. But this time, Moses went his own way in carrying out God's commands. Moses was to speak to the rock, but instead he struck it with his staff twice.

*"Wait...that's it? What's the big deal? God told Moses to strike the rock last time...what was different this time?"*

Well, God clarifies in verse 12: *"Because you did not believe in Me, to uphold Me as holy in the eyes of the people of Israel..."*

*"But couldn't God give Moses a break here? I mean, it's MOSES! He's been the most faithful out of everyone! Shouldn't he be allowed into the Promised Land?*

But look closely...what is God concerned about?

First, Moses' belief. Despite everything, he still wasn't perfect. He still had room to grow. Moses was to let his belief in God manifest in obeying God in *everything*.

Second, God cares about His name. His reputation. He is God and has authority. Whether Moses intentionally disobeyed God, was careless, or something else, the action didn't respect God's authority over him.

It's like when a child chooses to not clean their room after being told to. Regardless of their reasoning, the action displays, *"My parent's authority is not valuable enough for me to follow."*

Third, God was concerned about how the *people* saw Him. If *Moses* wouldn't be held accountable for his actions, why should they? God was holding Moses to a higher standard because he had authority over them.

Let's go to a school setting...if one student lashes out in anger at another student and punches them in the face, he will get in trouble. Perhaps a detention or suspension.

But now imagine if a teacher did that. They'd lose their job and have difficulty getting a new one. Why such a harsher consequence? Because teachers have authority and need to be held to a higher standard. I believe the same is happening with Moses here.

Moses was called to be an example of how to follow God. Let's look at the kind of leadership Jesus calls us to through some of the New Testament letters...

## SCRIPTURE

1 Timothy 3:1–7
Hebrews 13:17
James 3:1–6

## READ

In the context of 1 Timothy, Paul is talking about the character a man must have to become an elder. Why? Because they will be a picture of Christ to the rest of their local church. The church should be able to look at him and consistently think, *"I know how to better live for Christ because of how he lives his life."*

In Hebrews, we learn that these leaders will have to *"give an account"* for how they shepherded and took care of the church. Considering the marriage metaphor God uses, it'd be like God saying, *"How did you take care of my wife?"* Talk about an intense performance review!

And in James, we are actually warned about becoming teachers of God's Word. Now according to Matthew 28:18–19, *all* Christians are to teach others how to follow Jesus. But here we are talking about having a consistent teaching role in the lives of others. Teachers will also give an account with *"greater strictness."*

To break the fourth wall for a moment...this is why I've been praying over this study so much as I write it. One of my biggest prayers is, *"Lord, may my teaching be accurate, holy, and pleasing to You. May all that is inaccurate or unhelpful be removed or forgotten."*

These verses aren't to scare us away from becoming teachers or leaders, but to challenge us to not take God's Word lightly. Though not all will be elders, all are called to be people who match the character requirements. Though not all will be leaders, all are to teach His Word and have godly influence in their settings. Though not all are teachers, all are to "tame their tongue" that Jesus may be glorified.

In all things, we aren't to look at Moses as our *first* model of leadership, but to Christ Himself. **Jesus is the standard of character and illustration of a "tamed tongue" that we are to ultimately imitate.** Praise God for the wonderful example we have in Him!

## JOURNAL

**We are not sure whether Moses' response to strike the rock was intentional, absent-minded, or something else.** But it wasn't what God commanded. Are there any commands that you are half-heartedly obeying? Only partly obeying? That you haven't taken seriously? That you've perverted to suit your personality or lifestyle better? What impact might your disobedience be having? What impact would *full* obedience have? What are some ways you can more closely obey Christ from here on out?

**Though not all are called to be elders, we are certainly called to resemble the character traits listed in 1 Timothy 3:1–7.** Looking at that list again, what areas are you doing well in? What are some victories Christ has been having in you? What are some areas you could improve on?

**Jesus' command for all Christians is to teach others how to follow Him (Matthew 28:20).** Who are some believers you have influence over currently? How might you be intentional in pointing them to Jesus? Is there anyone God is asking you to specifically pour into? Anyone come to mind who could use your encouragement? Spend some time praying for that person. Take a risk to reach out to them. Invite them to grab a meal, and look for opportunities to share some wisdom in your conversation.

## CLOSING PRAYER

*"Lord, may I become more like You, my good Shepherd. May my character be like Yours. May my words be as if You Yourself were speaking through me in all things. May I have courage to teach and encourage others on their journey with You. Help me, Lord. I love You. Amen."*

# 48

# Moses' Farewell

## OPENING PRAYER

*"Here I am, Lord."*

## READ

After forty years of wandering in the wilderness, Moses stands before the people to give his final words before he dies. These speeches make up the majority of Deuteronomy.

**I'd like you to first read the entirety of Deuteronomy 6:1–9:5.** Go slowly, letting God's Word "marinate" over you as you read.

I have then broken it down into smaller passages with specific Journal questions for each. I'd encourage you to also move through these questions slowly. My hope is that you yourself will discover what God desires *for* His people and what He wants to do *through* His people, especially in light of all we have read through thus far.

## SCRIPTURE

Deuteronomy 6:1–9

## JOURNAL

- How are God's commandments and promises connected?
- What is the long-term desire God has for His people?

## SCRIPTURE

Deuteronomy 6:10–19

## JOURNAL

- What are unique ways that God will be providing for the Israelites?
- What threatens the Israelites to *"forget the LORD"*?

## SCRIPTURE

Deuteronomy 6:20–25

## JOURNAL

- What does the son's question imply about the life of their parent?
- What is to be the motivation for Israel's obedience?

## SCRIPTURE

Deuteronomy 7:1–11

## JOURNAL

- Seven is typically a number that symbolizes completeness in the Bible. What might be significant about "seven" in verse 1?
- Why is God adamant about the *"complete destruction"* of these peoples? When and why has He "completely destroyed" before?
- What is God's motivation for choosing Israel for His mission?

## SCRIPTURE

Deuteronomy 7:12–16

## JOURNAL

• What are the promises God is making **as part of His covenant with Israel**?

• How are these promises *different* than the promises Jesus makes in the new covenant? (Check out John 15:18–16:4.)

## SCRIPTURE

Deuteronomy 7:17–26

## JOURNAL

• Why is it significant that once again God starts with what *He* will do and then follows it with what the *Israelites* are to do?

• How does God temper the expectations of the Israelites in how quickly they will take the Promised Land? Why do you think He does this?

## SCRIPTURE

Deuteronomy 8:1–10

## JOURNAL

• What were the purposes for God testing the Israelites?

• How do you think the Israelites felt during the time of testing?

## SCRIPTURE

Deuteronomy 8:11–9:5

## JOURNAL

• Why do you think God promises that the Israelites will perish if they worship other gods?

• According to God, why is Israel driving out these nations?

## JOURNAL

After looking into Scripture and seeking to understand it more deeply, let's let the Scripture "read" us now...

**A huge theme of this passage is to remember what God has done.** What are some things you have forgotten that the Lord has done for you? How has He fought for you? Provided for you? Taken care of you? Comforted you? Blessed you? Tested you? Spend time thanking God for those things!

**God's blessing on the Israelites in this context is conditional based on their behavior and obedience to Him.** Though we are saved by grace, what are some ways we experience His blessings when we obey Him? How do we experience His discipline?

**Jesus quotes multiple verses from these passages in the New Testament.** Did you recognize any? (Maybe do a quick search online!) How did He use these verses? In what situations? How does Jesus model using Scripture in everyday life?

## CLOSING PRAYER

*"Lord, may I not forget You. May I remain faithful to You as You are faithful to me. Please, Lord. May You be praised. Amen."*

# THE CONQUEST ERA

# PART IV: THE CONQUEST ERA

## SUMMARY

*God fulfills a promise to a friend by giving his descendants land, intending it to be His base of operations towards redeeming the world.*

## THE SCRIPTURE OF THIS ERA

Joshua

## INTRODUCTION

God has fulfilled His first promise to Abraham, turning his descendants into the nation of Israel. He initiates the Mosaic Covenant, this divine partnership where He is to be their God and they are to be His people. He's told them how they are to run as a nation and live as a people distinct from the rest of the world that they may be a *"kingdom of priests"* inviting others to be reconciled with God.

At the end of the Exodus Era, Moses delivers his final words before walking up a mountain overlooking the Promised Land in Deuteronomy 34. God shows Him the land He will give his people, and Moses dies, buried by God Himself (Deuteronomy 34:5-6).

We've seen three forty-year periods of Moses' life with God. The first he was in Egypt, the second he was a shepherd on the run, and the third he was a shepherd over God's people. These final moments provide us with a tender scene between a man and his God who've been in each other's lives for 120 years (Deuteronomy 34:7).

And now, after forty years of wandering in the wilderness, it is finally time for God's people to enter the Promised Land.

This is where we get our name for the **Conquest Era.** The Israelites are on a *quest* to *conquer* the land God promised to give them.

God has **two clear goals** for this mission:

1. Deliver judgment on the Canaanites for the incredible evil they had been doing for hundreds of years.
2. Fulfill His promise to Abraham to give his descendants a land so that through them they may be a blessing to the rest of the world.

We'll spend next chapter discussing that first goal to set the stage before launching into the narrative.

The Conquest Era follows the journey of God conquering Canaan on behalf of Israel seen mostly through the eyes of Joshua. It will begin with Joshua's commission into leadership and finish with the end of his life as he reflects back on what God has done, calling Israel to finish the work God has set out for them to do.

# 49

# The Conquest of Canaan

## OPENING PRAYER

*"Lord Jesus, may You be glorified during this time. Please soften my heart to receive what You have for me. Please weaken my flesh that I may not rebel against Your goodness in this time. I love You, Lord. Amen."*

## READ

Many struggle with the violence God commands in this era. To be clear, *God is explicitly calling for the complete extermination of certain people groups, including women and children.*

You might be wondering, *"How can I reconcile this with the Jesus I know? And what are we as Christians to do with this?"*

Fortunately, the Bible has made God's intentions incredibly clear. I'd like to take this chapter to address this whole topic before jumping into the narrative, simply because I don't want it to be a distraction simmering in the background. Heads-up, this is going to be a longer chapter, so don't feel the need to complete it in one sitting. My hope is that these things won't make you squirm but actually cause you to rejoice in Jesus even more!

To frame our time, I will have you look at certain passages of Scripture and come to your own conclusions first. (We've looked at a couple of them already.) Then I will provide my thoughts and some responses to potential questions.

When we read passages like these, it can sometimes be hard to remember that Jesus and Yahweh are one and the same. To help us know Jesus better, I will intentionally be using Jesus' name to remind us that it is *He* who is initiating this conquest.

(Quick note: God will specify different tribes living in the region of Canaan, but for simplicity's sake, I will refer to them all as Canaanites.)

## SCRIPTURE

Genesis 15:13–21
Leviticus 18 (*Note: Due to explicit material, this passage might not yet be appropriate for younger kids.*)
Deuteronomy 7:1–6
Deuteronomy 8:17–20
Deuteronomy 20

## THINK

- *Where is His grace?*
- *Where is His lordship?*
- *How is God distinguishing the Canaanites from other nations?*

## READ

Here are six points I'd like to make to help us see Jesus' goodness and justice in this era.

**1) Jesus is patient with evil.** *"...the iniquity of the Amorites is not yet complete,"* God says in Genesis 15:16. Jesus was giving the Canaanites *plenty of time* to change their ways...about 500 years. In His mercy, He's actually *letting* them continue to carry out evil to give them more time to return to Him. This is good news, as Jesus has patiently waited for us to turn away from evil and return to Him! It's good news for our non-believing friends who have yet to surrender to Him...there's still time!

**2) Jesus *will* judge evil.** There comes a point when Jesus declares "enough is enough." He did it with the evil in Noah's day and with Pharaoh, and He's going to do it again when Jesus returns. There are a few things we know about the evil Canaan was committing. First, there was incredible sexual perversion. Leviticus 18 opens by telling the Israelites to not follow the practices of the Canaanites before laying them out specifically: incest, polygamy, adultery, homosexuality, and bestiality. God makes it clear that this is why He's judging them. A second thing we know from Deuteronomy 12:29–31 is that they also practiced child sacrifice, burning their children alive as a form of worship to their gods. It's good news that Jesus *will* put an end to evil! That He *hates* evil!

**3) What's happening here is *not* genocide, but judgment.** Some people try to make the claim the Israelites are carrying out a genocide on behalf of God. Hopefully, the previous point made it clear that Jesus is doing this due to Canaan's evil actions and not their ethnicity. But to prove the point further, we *will* see instances of Canaanites being allowed to become part of God's people because they put their faith in Yahweh (Joshua 2). One of them will even be in the ancestry of Jesus! This is good news because it reveals that God is not blind to the individuals' hearts! It's not simply sweeping judgment in the sense that *"because you are part of this people group, you are doomed."* It's specific as well. Praise God that we can trust He knows the hearts of those He judges! Praise Jesus *no one* will be unjustly judged by Him!

**4) Jesus' judgment is non-partial.** In Deuteronomy 8:20, Moses warns, *"Like the nations that the LORD makes to perish before you, so shall you perish, because you would not obey the voice of the LORD your God."* Jesus makes it clear that He will do the same to Israel if they follow the practices of the Canaanites. Praise God that He does not play favorites! Praise God He holds all to account! He is just and fair!

**5) Jesus' judgment is specific.** Deuteronomy 20 has a list of rules the Israelites are to abide by concerning warfare. It is here Jesus clarifies the complete extermination is reserved *only* for the Canaanites. *No one else.* Hopefully, you were also able to identify how good God is concerning these laws on war. That *He* will fight for His people. That He prioritizes homelife and marriages over governmental requirements to fight. That He allows the fearful to go home because He cares about the morale of His people. That He wants them *always* to offer peace first. That these conquered people will be subjected a nation called to love and bless the lowly, protecting them from abuse, standing in stark contrast to the surrounding brutal nations... God wants to use this system so that they can come to Him! That He spares the women, children, and animals of the nations led by foolish men who reject the peace God offers. That He doesn't want nature to be needlessly destroyed. How good Jesus is!

**6) Jesus is the one fighting against the Canaanites.** We will see this play out throughout the book of Joshua, but God promises it ahead of time in Deuteronomy 7:21–24. *He* is the one who will conquer them. *He* is the one bringing victory to the Israelites. Through a variety of miracles, God makes it clear that *He* is the one leading this conquest. Israel is only a tool in His hand, if you will. Praise God for His confirmation through miracles!

Now I want to address two "push-back" questions that come up during this conversation...

**Push-back #1:** *"Why does Jesus want the kids killed too? They're innocent!"* I've addressed this idea in the Passover chapter, but just in case you've forgotten...

a) **According to Scripture, no one is innocent and we are all born sinful** *(Romans 3:23; Romans 5:12; Psalm 51:5).* This includes kids of all ages, inside and outside the womb.

b) **Jesus knows the limited capacity some ages have in understanding repentance and the difference between right and wrong** *(1 Samuel 16:7; Jeremiah 20:12).* He is a judge who judges fairly in every circumstance. He will do what is right.

c) **David seemed to believe he would be with his dead child again** *(2 Samuel 12:23).* Though the Bible doesn't have a black-and-white statement on this topic, this passage leads me to believe that those who die in the womb or as infants are lovingly welcomed into Heaven by God. Even if Jesus is the initiator of their deaths, to me there is room to believe they could still be with Him.

d) **God doesn't want remaining Canaanites to lure the Israelites into sin**, as we've seen in multiple passages already. If the kids live, that means remnants of the culture will live. Jesus doesn't want His people influenced by them at all.

**Push-back #2:** *"But this doesn't seem fair! How would these people turn back to God if they grew up in a culture that doesn't know Him?"*

a) **The things happening in Egypt were not unknown to the Canaanites.** We will learn in Joshua 2 that they were *very* aware of the God of the Israelites, and they will be given the opportunity to surrender to Him.

**b) Romans 1:18–32** lays out how people like the Canaanites are still guilty of sin even if they don't know the Law, so I encourage you to read it yourself. But you can think of it this way: Imagine a person is driving 75 mph in a residential neighborhood, even though they saw the speed limit sign reading 35 mph. Do they deserve a ticket? Of course! But what about a person who *hasn't* seen the sign? Would *that* person deserve a ticket? Of course! They still broke the law, regardless if they knew about it or not. And the implications of Romans 1 is that even if that person doesn't know the exact speed limit, they still know deep down they shouldn't be driving that fast in a residential neighborhood. Everyone deep down knows they are a sinner.

In all of this, it is incredibly important that we realize that **the conquest of Canaan was a *specific judgment* from Jesus to be carried out by a *specific group of people* in a *specific time of history* for a *specific set of reasons*.**

Nowhere does Christ call Christians to carry out conquests like these today. You may have questions regarding a biblical response to war in general, but we will not address that at this moment. In the meantime, let's remember our current context under Christ's new covenant...

## SCRIPTURE

Ephesians 6:10–13
2 Peter 3:9–10

## JOURNAL

**2 Peter 3:2–9 talks about Jesus' return to judge the evil on earth.** How is God's judgment of Canaan a foreshadow of Christ's return? What are some similarities you see? What is *good* about what God is doing in this passage?

**Ephesians 6:10–13 talks about how we are to live in the middle of God's "slowness" and "patience" in 2 Peter 3:9.** With this in mind, how are we to navigate difficulties? How should we view those who oppose God's people? How should we view those who do great evil in the world? What should we do when we are persecuted for our faith? How did Jesus model this?

**Jesus is the one who sent the Israelites on this mission to conquer Canaan.** How does this challenge your view of Jesus? How might you need to adjust your view of Jesus? How might this truth need to alter the way you receive Jesus' commands over your life?

## CLOSING PRAYER

*"Jesus, You are holy. You are good and just. May I see You more as You are and not as I want You to be. Please correct my thinking and change my heart that I may rejoice in You in all things. I love You, Lord. To You only be the glory. Amen."*

# 50

# God Commissions Joshua

## OPENING PRAYER

*"Lord Jesus, You are good and You desire good for me. May I receive that good today. May I be changed, empowered, encouraged, and challenged by You that I may become more like You. I love You, Lord. Amen."*

## READ

Let's jump back into the narrative to see what God does next. We'll set it up with a few "flashbacks" in Exodus and Deuteronomy and then pick it up in Joshua...

## SCRIPTURE

Exodus 17:8–16
Deuteronomy 31:1–7
Deuteronomy 34:5–12
Joshua 1

## THINK

• *Where is His grace?*

*• Where is His lordship?*

*• What is consistently repeated in these passages? Why do you think that is? What might it imply?*

## READ

*Just a little background on what is going on in Joshua 1:12–15: Back in Numbers 21, the Israelites were seeking safe passage from two kings, Sihon and Og, while they were wandering in the wilderness, but the kings attacked them instead. So God gave the Israelites victory by conquering them. Later in Numbers 32, Reuben, Gad, and Manasseh (three of the twelve tribes of Israel) asked Moses if they could just settle in that conquered land. Moses agreed as long as they promised to help the other tribes complete the conquest for the actual Promised Land, which they did.*

A former slave in Egypt. A warrior against the Amalekites. An aide to Moses on Mt. Sinai. A spy who stood strong against his nation. One of two remaining men of his generation after forty years in the wilderness. And now the leader God has chosen for Israel.

All eyes are on Joshua now.

So the question put forth is, *"How will Joshua lead?"*

*Spoiler alert:* Joshua will be one of the few people in Scripture who starts strong and ends stronger. He won't be perfect, but he is certainly one to watch closely.

Over and over again, the book of Joshua repeats the refrain *"be strong and courageous."* Moses says this to Joshua in front of all Israel. God says it to him directly *three times.* And then the men he will be leading into battle encourage him as well.

We also see Moses wanting the victory over the Amalekites to be written down and recited specifically to Joshua. *"Remember this, Joshua!"* And Moses lays his hands on him, praying that the wisdom *he had* would be on Joshua.

Seeing all this, my hunch is that Joshua was not feeling *"strong and courageous."* Otherwise, it wouldn't have to be repeated so much! But God has chosen him for this task, regardless of how Joshua feels.

Joshua 1:1–9 highlights an important aspect of living with God:

*"Now therefore **arise, go**...into the land **I am giving** to them..."*

*"...every place that the **sole of your foot** will tread **I have given**..."*

*"...**you shall cause** this people to inherit the land that **I swore** to their fathers to give them."*

**God has promised an outcome, and yet it requires Joshua's obedience.** But how can this be? Are God's promises *truly* contingent upon the faithful actions of a person?

This is one of those mysteries about God that is outside our capacity of understanding. Somehow, yes, God never breaks a promise *and* He commands unreliable people to fulfill those promises.

The point is not to focus on *how* this is possible but *our response* in this reality. **Joshua was encouraged by Moses to fulfill his mission to conquer Canaan. In the New Testament, Timothy was encouraged by Paul to fulfill his mission of sharing the good news of Jesus...**

## SCRIPTURE

2 Timothy 1:1–14
2 Timothy 3:14–4:5

## JOURNAL

**As Moses poured into Joshua's life, Timothy was poured into by his mother, grandmother, and Paul.** Are you allowing more mature Christians to pour *specifically* into you *in person*? (We're not talking about online influencers here.) If so, who are they? How have you been shaped by them? What do you admire about their faith? If you aren't, how come? How might you grow if you did? Are *you* pouring into anyone right now? (Remember, those people can be your kids!) Why or why not?

**Both Timothy and Joshua received gifts from God as a result of their mentors laying their hands on them in prayer.** If you have a mentor, how often do you go to them for prayer? Have you allowed them to *really* speak into your life? Into the things you are uncomfortable with? Decide now to let them bless you by letting them speak into those things.

**Both Timothy and Joshua were encouraged to not walk in fear but in power and courage.** Are you walking in fear? Would you describe yourself as a timid person? Where does God want Joshua to get his courage from? Where does God want Timothy to get his courage from? What would it look like for you to be *"strong and courageous"* and to walk in *"power and love and self-control"*?

**God acknowledges He will fulfill His promises through Joshua. Paul acknowledges that God has appointed us with a *"holy calling"* that was appointed *"before the ages began."*** And both Joshua and Timothy were called to walk faithfully in those callings. How can this "destined" calling on your life to share the gospel of Jesus empower you to be faithful in it?

**Both Joshua and Timothy were called to really *abide in* and *know* God's Word.** Why is that so important? What are God's hopes for you? What are the benefits God lists out? Are you careful to do all God commands you to do in His Word? Are you not turning from His Word *"to the right hand or to the left"*? Are you constantly speaking His Word out loud? Are you meditating on His Word day and night? Are you being taught by His Word? Reproofed (rebuked) and corrected by His Word? Are you training in His Word? Preaching His Word? Ready with His Word? Reproving, rebuking, and exhorting others with His Word?

## CLOSING PRAYER

*"Lord Jesus, You are the Word. May I know You more deeply and intimately. May I live and walk in Your power, love, and self-control. May I be strong and courageous in all I do because You are with me. I love You, Lord. Amen."*

# Rahab & the Spies

## OPENING PRAYER

*"Jesus, may I glorify You today. May my words, actions, and thoughts be pleasing to You. Would You please use this time in Your Word to make me more like You? I need You. I love You. Amen."*

## SCRIPTURE

Joshua 2

## THINK

- *Where is His grace?*
- *Where is His lordship?*
- *What is God doing in Rahab's life?*
- *What is God doing in Joshua's life?*

## READ

Joshua sends two spies into Jericho, the first target of the conquest. (Notice how he only sent two instead of twelve? The motivation isn't made clear, but we may have some fair guesses...)

Now what has been repeated over and over again to Joshua before this?

*"Be strong and courageous..."*

And now Joshua learns from the spies that the people of Jericho are *terrified*. They heard about what God did to Egypt. To the Red Sea. To Sihon and Og. And even though it happened forty years ago, the people of Jericho are melting in fear. Why?

*Because that nation of God has now marched to their doorstep.*

I believe God was being merciful to Joshua here. He didn't *have* to give him this information. He could have had Joshua just go forth relying on His promises alone. But instead, God chooses to pull back the curtain of what He's been up to with Jericho. He reveals Jericho's fear to encourage Joshua even more so. What an amazing, generous God!

And then we see His mercy and love toward Rahab. Remember all the reasons why God is judging Canaan? Well, as a Canaanite prostitute, likely used and abused in the heart of worship toward their gods, Rahab squarely fits the bill for destruction.

And yet, her response to Yahweh is different than her people's. She humbles herself, acknowledges that He is Lord, and puts her faith immediately into action. She risks her life to protect two Israelite men by lying to the king of her people. (Perhaps you remember two other women who risked their lives by lying to the king to protect some other Hebrew boys...) Yahweh is her new King.

Because of her faith, God invites her to be part of His family. It's the first piercings of light that God will fulfill His third promise to Abraham. That through His people, there is hope for the rest of the world to be reconciled to Him.

God will count Rahab's faith among those like Noah, Abraham, and Moses in Hebrews 11:31. And Jesus Himself will have some Canaanite blood in Him with Rahab as one of His ancestors (Matthew 1:5). What a beautiful turn in this woman's life! All due to God's grace of receiving Rahab's active faith.

## SCRIPTURE

James 2:14–26
Hebrews 11:1–2

## READ

Many have misunderstood the passage in James to mean that in order to be saved, you have to have faith in Jesus *and* do good works. If that were the case, then Christ's sacrifice would've been insufficient to save us. But when Jesus said *"It is finished"* in John 19:30, I think He meant it.

However, some try to say that mere "belief" in what Jesus has done is enough. And James' point is that believing a fact is not enough. The demons believe Jesus died for our sins!

So what shall distinguish us from the demons? It's the *response* that comes from that belief. The demons believe and respond in further rebellion, as do many! James is trying to communicate that faith *means* belief in righteous action.

Hebrews frames it as *"assurance of things hoped for, the conviction of things not seen."* When one has conviction, they act accordingly to that belief. You would never consider a criminal to have a strong conviction for the justice system, even if he proclaimed he did. Why? Because their actions don't line up with their beliefs.

The same could be said for the Christian. You wouldn't consider a person who never obeys the commands of Jesus a Jesus-follower, even if they said they were.

If there are no good works or obedience to Jesus' commands, it's probably an indicator that person doesn't truly have faith, and therefore has no salvation.

Good works and action are the *follow-through* of true faith. They are evidences of someone's salvation. And this is exactly what Rahab practiced and is commended for in James.

## JOURNAL

**Joshua only sent two spies into Canaan rather than twelve like Moses did.** Though we can only guess his reasoning, we see he certainly is distinguishing his decision from Moses'. When was a time you made a decision intentionally different than someone else's? What motivated you to make that change? How did it pan out? What lessons have you taken to heart from experiences others have had?

**Jericho was *terrified* of the God of Israel.** Was there ever a time *you* were terrified of God like they were? Maybe before you became a Christian? Do you feel afraid of God now? What's causing that fear? If you are feeling afraid of God, be courageous to share that with someone. Ask them for input on why that is. Ask the Holy Spirit to remind you of His love for you and the kind of relationship He desires with you.

**I believe God pulled back the curtain for Joshua to see what He's been doing in Jericho to encourage him.** When were some times that Jesus did that with His disciples? Has He ever revealed things to you so you could be encouraged or comforted?

## CLOSING PRAYER

*"Lord, may my life be operated out of deeper and deeper conviction of You. Of Your grace, Your power, and Your gospel. May my faith grow and glorify You. Be close to me, Lord. I love You. Amen."*

52

# Crossing the Jordan

## OPENING PRAYER

*"Heavenly Father, You know my needs. May I receive provision through Your Word today. Amen."*

## SCRIPTURE

Joshua 3–4

## THINK

- *Where is His grace?*
- *Where is His lordship?*
- *What parallels do you see between Joshua and Moses?*

## READ

For the past two chapters, we've been looking at how for decades God had been preparing Joshua for this mission. And it seems that Joshua has taken the message to *"be strong and courageous"* fully to heart. Like Abraham, Joshua rises early in the morning to obey God's commands.

And now that Joshua is ready, God turns His attention to the people. In His great wisdom, God prepares the leader first *and then* the people.

For decades, God had been displaying His great power and presence with Moses. But surely the people had questions about how things would go with this "new Moses."

*"Will Yahweh be with Joshua? Are we on our own? Will God abandon us now that Moses is gone…?"* I believe God was using this event as a definitive answer to those questions for His people.

He begins as He often does by establishing *Himself* as the true Leader and King of Israel. His "royal throne" of the Mercy Seat atop the Ark of the Covenant is carried forward by the Levites about a half-mile in front of the people. *He* is the one leading them into battle.

They arrive at the border of the Jordan River during flood season and, like at the Red Sea, God miraculously parts the water. Likely over two million people with their animals, tents, and goods crossed the river on dry ground. *Every single one of them* experienced this miracle. And my hunch is that *every single one* passed by Joshua as they did so.

*"Today I will begin to exalt you in the sight of all Israel, that they may know that, as I was with Moses, so I will be with you,"* God says to Joshua.

And then He fulfills His promise like He always does. *"On that day the LORD exalted Joshua in the sight of all Israel, and they stood in awe of him just as they had stood in awe of Moses, all the days of his life."*

It would be in this same river nearly 1,400 years later when God would exalt a new Leader for His people…

## SCRIPTURE

Mark 1:9–15

## READ

Jesus had been living in relative obscurity up until this point, but now He was to launch His public ministry. He meets his cousin John "the Baptizer" at the Jordan River to be baptized by him. And when He comes up out of the water, we get a unique moment in Scripture when all three members of the Trinity are specifically distinguished and identified together.

The people at the Jordan don't witness a miraculous parting of water to highlight God's presence with Jesus. Instead, they get an audible declaration of God Himself saying, *"You are my beloved Son; with You I am well pleased."* Can't get more definitive than that!

And instead of the Ark of the Covenant representing God's presence in the middle of the Jordan, the Holy Spirit *Himself* shows up on the scene, descending not onto the Mercy Seat but onto *Jesus Himself. Jesus* is the "new Ark of the Covenant."

Hopefully you noticed the parallel of Jesus' forty days of testing in the wilderness with the forty years of testing the Israelites experienced. But Jesus passes His tests with flying colors (Matthew 4:1–11).

And then we get an incredible picture of Jesus as the "better Joshua" when He starts proclaiming the gospel:

*"The time is fulfilled, and the kingdom of God is at hand…"*

**Just as God's appointed time for Israel's taking of the land had come, God's appointed time for Christ's taking of the earth has come.**

*"...repent and believe in the gospel."*

Every nation the Israelites approach will have the opportunity to surrender, as Rahab did. And now everyone whom Jesus approaches will have the opportunity to surrender to Him.

**Joshua led the establishment of Israel in Canaan through war. Jesus established His Kingdom over the earth through sacrificial love—though when He returns, it will be completed in a final war against evil.**

To take this comparison one step further, let us consider Joshua's name...*Joshua* is the English transliteration of the Hebrew name *Yeshua,* which means "Yahweh saves."

Do you know what the Greek transliteration is?

*Jesus.*

## JOURNAL

**God commands that twelve stones be taken from the middle of the Jordan River to memorialize this event for both the people then and for the coming generations.** Why is it that personal testimonies are so impactful? What is a testimony from someone that has had a great impact on you? How are *you* memorializing what God has done in your life for *your* future generations? (Or for future generations in general?) How might you encourage them and provide testimonies of His goodness and power?

**Joshua 3:11 and 4:24 highlight God's authority over the whole world and His desire for the whole world to know Him.** If you let this reality sink in more, how might it affect your view on ministry work? On sharing the gospel? On your prayer life? On your openness to being sent by Him? On generosity toward other churches? How real for you is it that Jesus is the true *Lord* of the *entire world*? Or is your thinking limited to your immediate context?

**God intentionally exalted Joshua in the eyes of the people for the work ahead.** Is *Jesus* exalted in your eyes? Are you truly in awe of Him? Do you feel the weight of His authority over your life? Do you feel the weight of His presence *with* you? Are you encouraged and empowered by His presence to follow *Him* into "spiritual warfare"?

## CLOSING PRAYER

*"Jesus, thank You for all the ways it has been confirmed that You are the Son of God. May You become even more glorious and beautiful in my eyes. May I walk obediently in Your footsteps. To You only be the glory. Amen."*

# 53

# Preparing for War

## OPENING PRAYER

*"Jesus, may You be magnified in this time. May I fall more in love with You. Amen."*

## SCRIPTURE

Joshua 5

## THINK

- *Where is His grace?*
- *Where is His lordship?*

## READ

Israel has just crossed the Jordan River. The land is before them. The nations are *terrified*. And what does God have them do?

Mutilate all their men. Sort of...

Back in Genesis 17:1–14, as part of the Abrahamic Covenantal agreement, Abraham and his male descendants were to be circumcised. (For my younger readers, it's a specific surgery for boys. If you want to make your parents uncomfortable, ask them.)

Circumcision was meant to serve as a sign to say, *"I belong to the God of Abraham and His promises."* It's sort of like wearing a wedding ring to say, *"I belong to my spouse and our marriage covenant."* Circumcision doesn't mean you're automatically part of the covenant, just as simply putting on a wedding ring doesn't magically make you married. But they are both meant to serve as powerful signs.

Putting on a wedding ring and being circumcised as a grown man in the middle of the desert with a flint knife, however, are two very different things.

Think about how vulnerable Israel was during this time! *All* of the fighting men undergoing intense surgery and needing to heal for what could be weeks. It would have been a perfect moment for the Canaanites to attack if they hadn't been so afraid!

**God was intentionally calling Israel to become weak so that His strength would be evident.** Israel had to trust God *big time* in this moment. God is driving home the point that this is *His* battle to fight, not theirs. And that **they belong to Him, not themselves.**

After **submitting** their strength to God, the Israelites are called to **remember** what God has done by observing Passover. God wants them to **be strengthened** because of *His* faithfulness.

To drive this point across even further, God stops providing manna. The Israelites will now **have to depend** on God's victory if they want to survive. And the only way for them to receive the food and blessings of the Promised Land is for them to **take it**.

And then there's the commander of the army of the Lord...

Some believe this was an angel. I personally believe this was a **Christophany, a pre-incarnate appearance of Jesus Himself**. ("Pre-incarnate" refers to the existence of Jesus before He was born of Mary.)

For one, the last time someone took their sandals off because they were standing on holy ground was when Moses was before God at the burning bush in Exodus 3:5.

Also, when Joshua bows down to worship, the commander doesn't stop him. In Revelation 22:8–9, John bows to worship an angel and the angel responds, *"You must not do that! I am a fellow servant...Worship God."* This leads me to believe Joshua was in the presence of Jesus Himself.

And Jesus makes something very clear to Joshua. **This conquest is not between Israel and their enemies. It's between God and *His* enemies.** Let there be no mistake.

## SCRIPTURE

Ephesians 6:10–20
2 Corinthians 12:7–10

## READ

Though you and I aren't part of a conquest like Joshua, Jesus still demands we have a correct perspective on the spiritual war we *are* in.

In Ephesians, we are reminded that **our battle is not "Christians versus the world." It's "Christ versus the spiritual forces of evil."**

We are part of this war because we are in Christ. Not through circumcision, but through faith in Christ and His sacrifice. **We belong to Christ, not ourselves.**

In 2 Corinthians, God reveals that at times He may intentionally subject us to spiritual warfare for our benefit. To prevent Paul from becoming arrogant about all he has done for Christ, God allows a *"messenger of Satan"* to harass him regularly. **God was intentionally calling Paul to become weak so that *His* strength would be evident.**

And what's Paul's response? Praising Jesus!

He **surrenders** to Christ, implicitly **remembering** what Christ has done for him and **is strengthened** to endure *"weaknesses, insults, hardships, persecutions, and calamities."*

He rejoices that he will **have to depend** on Christ's victory in order to be faithful in **taking** "spiritual ground" in the fight against evil, sharing the gospel in whatever circumstance.

And we are called to do the same.

## JOURNAL

**Both Paul and this new generation of Israelites went all in on Christ's mission.** Are you all in on Christ's mission? How would you describe your passion to share the gospel? What are you willing to sacrifice for it? Is there anything you *aren't* willing to sacrifice for it? Is there a "new level" of surrender God is calling you to right now? Are there any ways God is calling you to greater weakness so that His greater strength may be displayed?

**Look at the individual pieces of the "armor of God" again in Ephesians 6:10–20.** All of the items except for the *"sword of the Spirit"* are defensive in nature. Why do you think that is? What do you think it means to fasten on the *"belt of truth"*? To *"put on the breastplate of right-eousness"*? To wear the *"shoes"* of *"readiness given by the gospel of peace"*? To *"take up the shield of faith"*? To wear the *"helmet of salvation"*? To take up the *"sword of the Spirit, which is the word of God"*?

**We are in a spiritual war.** How aware of this are you on a regular basis? Do you live with a "warfare mindset"? What would it look like if you did? How would it affect the way you handle sin? Your urgency for the gospel? Your longing for Heaven?

## CLOSING PRAYER

*"Lord, thank You for going before me. Thank You for inviting me to weakness so that I may see Your strength on display. May my heart more sincerely hunger for You to be magnified in all I do. Amen."*

# 54

# The Fall of Jericho

## OPENING PRAYER

*"Lord, please grant me eyes to see You today. Please grant me ears to hear from You today. And may I respond in faith. I love You, my God. Amen."*

## SCRIPTURE

Hebrews 11:30

Joshua 6

## THINK

- *Where is His grace?*
- *Where is His lordship?*
- *Why do you think God completed this miracle the way He did?*

## READ

Imagine you are a soldier in Jericho. Your city is on lockdown. No one comes in, and no one goes out. You've heard about the desolation of Egypt—slain by hail and famine, an entire generation of boys dropping dead overnight, and the land plundered by a new nation of slaves.

You've heard about this nation somehow crossing the Red Sea on dry ground while the entire Egyptian army was washed away in an instant. About the brutal defeat of two nearby kings, Sihon and Og. You've heard that this new nation somehow crossed over the nearby Jordan River on dry ground. And now when you peer over your city walls...

There they are.

You hear seven, loud resounding horns as they approach. But they don't charge forward in attack.

They walk.

In complete silence.

The footsteps of a silent army thunder underneath the blaring trumpets as they slowly make their way around your city walls. You look to your fellow soldiers. They are shaking in utter dismay.

But then the horns begin to quiet, and the footsteps begin to soften.

*They're...leaving?!*

You peer over the wall's ledge as the army marches back to their camp.

*What...?*

But it turns out they haven't abandoned their mission. They return the next day, and just like the day before, they merely march around the walls and leave.

They do this for six days. Not a word. Just horns and footsteps.

But on the seventh day, something different happens. They keep marching...

And marching.

Seven times they march around the city. You can't watch anymore. You shrink down and cover your eyes and your ears.

And then the marching stops.

It's quiet. All you hear is your own breathing and your heart pounding in your chest. You know they are still out there. *What's hap-?*

The trumpets suddenly blare again, but this time it's followed by the roar of tens of thousands of men. It's deafening.

You hardly notice the floor underneath you quivering...shaking...violently. Loud cracks of stone bombard your ears around you. Dust floods your vision as the terrified screams of your comrades pierce through noise for a brief moment before they are buried in collapsing rock.

The floor then suddenly gives out beneath you, dropping you down into a pit of rubble that now crushes against you until everything goes dark...

## READ

Using your imagination while reading Scripture can be very beneficial. It can help you remember that these are real stories of real people in real locations experiencing real things. And they tend to stick with us better. Like the example above, putting yourself in the shoes of *anyone* in the stories we read can also give us a new perspective of what is going on.

Now our imagination is not inerrant (without flaw) like the Bible, so we need to hold it loosely. For instance, in my example I'm not *absolutely certain* there were soldiers on the walls because it is not specified in Scripture.

But we *do* know there were people living *inside* the walls because that's where Rahab lived. With that in mind, perhaps it would be interesting to imagine being a *family* witnessing the events above. Or maybe even the king of Jericho witnessing it from afar.

Again, we hold these loosely and don't base our theology off them. But we present our imagination to the Lord and ask the Holy Spirit to help us see as He sees.

What we certainly see in this passage is Jesus providing Joshua with how this takeover of Jericho will go down. And the Israelites follow His commands perfectly, their faith highlighted alongside Moses and Rahab's in Hebrews 11.

Despite the horns and threats of attack for six days, Jericho doesn't surrender. They could have like Rahab did! But they stubbornly don't. God ramps up the tension on day seven, but even then, there is no "white flag." And so God destroys the walls, sending the Israelite soldiers in to destroy everything and everyone.

Except Rahab, of course. Her home must not have fallen in the destruction, and the soldiers identify it by the scarlet cord tied to her window. As a result of this red mark on her home, the destruction "passes over" her, and this unlikely woman is spared.

Jesus Himself will also have a powerful interaction with an unlikely Canaanite woman...

## SCRIPTURE

Matthew 15:21–28

## READ

*"Wait, I thought the Israelites were supposed to destroy all the Canaanites. How is there one here 1,400 years later??"*

Well, there's your spoiler alert. But we'll get to that another time...

A woman with a demon-oppressed daughter comes to Jesus and begs Him for help. This seems like the sort of thing that Jesus would be happy to do, but He...ignores her? What is going on here?

Let's remember that Jesus knows everything, including what He is about to do. He does heal her daughter, so this initial rejection must be on purpose.

First, Jesus is clarifying His mission. Yes, He came out of love for the whole world (John 3:16), but having limited Himself in space and time, Jesus had to pick and choose when and how to spend His time. Because Jesus is ultimately the fulfillment of all God was doing through the Abrahamic and Mosaic covenants, His focus was on the Jewish people. The Gentiles (non-Jews) would be next.

The Jews were His chosen people. His family. And so He was focusing on His family first. To clarify, the word Jesus used for "dog" wouldn't be an insult in the same way we might take it today. It would be used to refer to a beloved domestic pet, which, though loved by a parent, would be prioritized after the children.

This still may sound harsh to you, but we must keep in mind the entire exchange. Jesus ends up commending the remarkable faith this Canaanite woman is displaying...in front of whom?

The disciples who were trying to send her away. Jesus is making a point to them and to her.

Jesus does love and welcome everyone, even the "enemies" of His people. It is by faith in Him that we may see miraculous healings. And it is by faith in Him that we are saved.

## JOURNAL

**Using our imagination while reading the Bible can reveal beautiful truths about God.** How did the retelling I provided strike you? Any ways you saw God differently? This story differently? Do any other stories come to mind that you'd want to try this technique on?

**Hebrews 11:30 commended the faith of a large group of people rather than just Joshua.** Are you part of a group that would be commended for their faith? Why or why not? How might that group grow to become that? *Could* that group become that? Do you need to change which groups you are a part of?

**The disciples were trying to send the Canaanite woman away.** Is there anyone you have dismissed recently that Jesus wouldn't have? Anyone you are unwilling to help? How come? How might you learn from what Jesus was teaching his disciples in this scenario?

## CLOSING PRAYER

*"Lord, would You grant me a holy imagination. Please awaken my mind, creativity, and curiosity to engage with Your Word more deeply. May I receive Your great wisdom and insight, Lord. I love You. Amen."*

# 55

# Achan & Ai

## OPENING PRAYER

*"Lord Jesus, thank You for this time together. I love You, Lord. May You be glorified. Amen."*

## SCRIPTURE

Joshua 6:16–19
Joshua 7–8

## THINK

- *Where is His grace?*
- *Where is His lordship?*
- *What are the various methods God uses to accomplish His purposes?*

## READ

Such crushing defeat at Ai after a resounding victory over Jericho completely unwound Joshua. Like his generation that perished in the wilderness, he accuses God of evil and longs not for Egypt but for the wilderness. We now understand a reason why he was so often told to *"be strong and courageous."*

At the same time, we *do* see a distinction in his cries to God that resembles Moses' cries. He calls upon God's character and His desire to make *His* name great among all the nations.

But then God snaps him out of it. It's almost as if God is saying, *"Get up! Stop wallowing! You're not thinking about this correctly! You've got work to do! Let's go!"* And to Joshua's great credit, once his perspective is adjusted, he gets up early in the morning to obey.

In fact, he *completely* locks back in to do what God wants him to do.

He follows God's leading to cast lots (think rolling dice) to identify the secret traitor Achan, destroying him and all he has. He heeds God's encouragement to not fear or be dismayed, completely following the military plans God provides to ambush Ai. Like Moses over the Amalekites, he stretches out his javelin toward the city until it's completely plundered and destroyed. And he remembers to obey Moses' commands back in Deuteronomy 27 to build an altar on Mount Ebal, write the Law on it, read it to the people, and lead them in a pronouncement of blessings and curses.

It's a picture of Joshua's remarkable character. He has a moment of weakness and "reversion" to an old way of thinking, but he doesn't stay there. **He isn't ruled by his emotions and fears but subjects them to the truth God provides and the actions God demands of him. And then he refuses to stop until his obedience is complete.**

He reminds us of our "better Joshua," Jesus, when He asked His Father to *"remove this cup"* from Him in Luke 22:39–44, a passage we've looked at before. Once Jesus confirmed that the cross *was* the only way, He subjected His emotions to an even greater, unwavering obedience.

**Joshua chose "locked-in" obedience once his emotions were corrected. Jesus chose "locked-in" obedience *even though* His emotions were validated!**

But let's not allow Achan to slip under the radar...

Achan was one of God's people, under the Law, and part of the nation God was trying to bless. And he traded that for a jacket and some cash. As a direct result of his disobedience, thirty-six people died.

Understand that God *wasn't* punishing thirty-six people for some other dude's sin. That would be unjust. What He *was* doing was letting them suffer the consequences of their actions.

God had been very clear that He would not be with them in their efforts if they rebelled. And when they did, He let them proceed in their own power to experience what happens when they do. (It's another confirmation that *He* is the one leading the conquest.)

It's similar to a football player getting ejected from a game because he was talking back to the refs. Only that player is punished, but the rest of the team suffers the natural consequences of his absence.

God takes sin incredibly seriously and calls us to root it out of our lives. In some cases, this may mean removing the influence of certain people in our lives as well...

## SCRIPTURE

1 Corinthians 6:9–11

1 Corinthians 5:9–13
Matthew 18:15–17

## READ

Paul says in 1 Corinthians 6:9–11 that those who aren't in right standing with God won't be going to Heaven. And the evidence for some is that they intentionally practice the sins he lists. They're **unrepentant**.

He goes on to distinguish them from those who *used to intentionally practice* these things but have since **repented** to Christ. Though they obviously still sin (as we all do!), in Christ they are *"washed"*, sanctified, and justified.

Perhaps you yourself are *intentionally* walking in one of the sinful practices listed. This is Paul's way of proving it is not too late to be made right with God! Jesus loves you so much that He died for you. And He invites you now to receive His forgiveness, be made clean, and walk differently with Him in love!

Until someone *has* repented, there *is* a distinction between the Christian (the *"brother"* in Matthew 18 and 1 Corinthians 5) and the non-Christian (*"those outside"* in 1 Corinthians 5). And Christians *are* to have different expectations with non-Christians than each other.

Followers of Jesus are eager to repent because they know Jesus' love for them and wish to love Him more fully. They might be stubborn at first, which is why Jesus says in Matthew 18 that it might take a few tries for them to come to their senses.

But if they don't, we are to treat these professing "Christians" as unbelievers. Jesus says to *"let him be to you as a Gentile and a tax collector."*

Jesus intentionally *loved* and *spent time with* those sorts of people with the hopes that they *would* still repent! But His intimacy with them was different than with His followers.

These professing "Christians" shouldn't be considered a follower of Jesus to you. They aren't a "Christian with a different perspective on things." We don't bend the truth of Scripture to accommodate their worldview. We seek to love them well while at the same time seek ways to remove their influence on us and other believers.

Achan's unrepentant sin led to devastating consequences for God's people. And the unrepentant sin of people who claim to follow Jesus will too.

## JOURNAL

**Joshua still struggled with the sinful worldviews and habits of his generation.** Consider your generation *(Baby Boomer, Gen X, Millennial, Gen Z, Gen Alpha...).* What are some distinct perspectives and habits your generation has compared with others? Which ones do you personally relate with? Which of these traits are good and godly? What unhealthy characteristics of your generation do you carry? What are healthy ways you have broken away from your generation?

**On his way toward obtaining God's blessings, Joshua encountered a setback that caused him to spiral.** When was a time you "spiraled" on your way toward God's blessing? Or when was a time you encountered a setback that you responded poorly to? If you had a "Jesus perspective" during that time, what might've been different? Are you currently experiencing a setback? What truths from God might require you to change your mindset? (If you don't know, ask a godly friend!)

**Like He did with Joshua, sometimes God just tells us to snap out of it and stand up.** Have you ever had a moment like that? Is He possibly telling you to do that in your current situation? What would it look like for you to rule over your emotions and "lock in" to obedience?

**Jericho's spoils were meant for God. Ai's were meant for the people.** Achan was impatient to receive blessings from God, so he chose the blessings *over* God. Things were out of order in his life. Are you prioritizing God's blessings over Him *Himself*? Are you focused on getting things *from* God rather than building your relationship *with* God? If so, confess this to Him and ask Him to mercifully change your heart to love Him more.

## CLOSING PRAYER

*"Lord Jesus, You were obedient to the point of death on a cross. May I be so too. Thank You for knowing my thoughts and feelings more clearly than I even know them. May I respond to Your kindness with full and eager obedience. In Your glorious name, amen."*

# 56

# The Gibeonite Deception

## OPENING PRAYER

*"Lord Jesus, please be close to me during this time. You know the things that weigh on my heart and mind. You know the distractions and the things vying for my attention. Help me fix my eyes on You, Jesus. I need You. Amen."*

## SCRIPTURE

Joshua 9

## THINK

- *Where is His grace?*
- *Where is His lordship?*
- *If you had been in Joshua's position, how would you have responded to the Gibeonites' arrival?*

## READ

Both Rahab and the Gibeonites surrendered to the Israelites. But Ruth placed her faith in Yahweh. The Gibeonites didn't. They acknowledged God's power and His presence with the Israelites, but they lacked the proclamation of faith that Rahab made.

This is confirmed when verse 15 specifically states that the Israelites *"did not ask counsel from the LORD."* It insinuates that Joshua had just made a huge mistake.

The Gibeonites were supposed to be wiped out to prevent the Israelites from adopting their practices, but now they just swore on behalf of Yahweh that they wouldn't!

So now what? Should they break the covenant and dishonor God's name in the face of the world in order to obey Him? Or should they honor the covenant, keeping God's reputation intact while disobeying His commands?

It seems that they're caught in a catch-22, a lose-lose situation with no clear next step. We're not told God's perspective on which action was the correct one at that point—only that they did not seek His counsel first. Maybe God *would have* approved the covenant with the Gibeonites despite their deception. We don't know. What we *will* find out in future stories is that there will be consequences for both sparing the Gibeonites *and* for breaking their covenant with them...

When Joshua didn't seek discernment from God, he was deceived by some actors in raggedy clothing. We are just as susceptible to deception as Joshua, but we *do* have one major advantage...

The Holy Spirit.

## SCRIPTURE

1 John 4:1–6

## READ

Make no mistake, there are people empowered by Satan who are trying to deceive you. It may be unintentional due to the fact that they themselves have already bought his lies and are just passing it along. It may be highly intentional through social media, social pressure, or small talk. We are called to be constantly on guard against Satan's lies and deceptive influence.

But if it's through deception, how could we possibly identify it?! Satan has been studying the human mind for thousands of years! He knows what makes us tick, our histories, our shame, our insecurities, our thoughts, our passions, our fears...*what hope do we possibly have?*

The Holy Spirit.

The Spirit of truth lives in us. We know Him, John reassures us. And the more we walk with Him, studying His Word and practicing obedience, the more we know Him. And the more we know Him, the more we know what *isn't* Him.

Imagine you receive a text from an unknown number asking for money. If they claim to be an acquaintance, you're more likely to be deceived. But if they claim to be your best friend, you'll know fairly quickly whether that's true or not. It's the same with Jesus.

This is why building your relationship with Jesus *through His Word* is the most important thing you can do (after surrendering your life to Him in the first place).

**Meditating on Scripture and letting the truth about who Jesus *is* and not who you *think* He is or *want* Him to be will keep you from being deceived.**

And unlike Joshua, we have the Holy Spirit living inside of us to help! Take a moment to let that sink in...

The God of the universe lives inside of you.

The God who created existence dwells with you.

The God who founded truth abides in you.

That is not merely a comforting feeling. If you are in Christ, that is truth.

So seek Him.

## JOURNAL

**Joshua did not seek God's counsel on a big decision he had.** When was a time you didn't either? What were the consequences? What do you think God *might've* told you? Are you seeking Christ's input on your current decisions? Do you have parameters on what you ask God about? (For example, you're comfortable asking Him about how to give money but not about a potential romantic partner.)

**The Gibeonites were allowed to live and serve as** *"cutters of wood and drawers of water for the congregation and for the altar of the LORD..." (Joshua 9:26–27).* Did you notice who the Gibeonites were to be serving? The people as a whole and more specifically the Levites. If the Israelites continued to be faithful to God, how might that impact the Gibeonites? Consider the non-Christians you are with regularly who might have less status or privileges than you...how might your faithfulness affect them? How might you invite them to be a part of what you're doing so that you can be a light to them?

*"By this you know the Spirit of God: every spirit that confesses that Jesus Christ has come in the flesh is from God..."* **(1 John 4:2).** Jesus Christ is both fully human *and* fully man. How do other religions reject that fact? (If you don't know, do a little digging.) Since they don't confess that truth, what does this mean about every other religion/belief? You have the truth of God living inside you...how can that inform your urgency to share the gospel? Who you go to for advice? How you talk about world affairs? How you are to love non-believers?

## CLOSING PRAYER

*"Lord, may I be faithful to You in all things. May I know You more so that I might not be deceived and so dishonor You. Please help me remember You and Your wisdom. Grant me the humility to submit to You when I do. I love You, Lord. Amen."*

# 57

# The Battle of the Five Kings

## OPENING PRAYER

*"Lord, I submit myself to You. May my heart not be stubborn or hard against You in this time. But may I grow soft at Your call that I may be conformed more into Your likeness. I love You, Jesus. Amen."*

## SCRIPTURE

Joshua 10

## THINK

- *Where is His grace?*
- *Where is His lordship?*
- *Joshua is now telling his men to "not be afraid or dismayed" and to "be strong and courageous" in verse 25. What do you think is going on inside Joshua that leads him to charge his men this way?*

## READ

Hailstones hurled down to kill. A spirit of panic. The sun miraculously frozen in the sky to ensure it continues to happen until all are dead. Bloodshed. Beheadings. Hanging corpses…

Maybe you're someone who enjoys these sorts of stories and these battles are epic adventures to you. If so, let them spur you on toward faithfulness! Even though your battles will look different, choose to be like Joshua and these courageous men. Re-read verses 29–43 slowly, meditating on their obedience and resolve to *completely* obey God while depending on *His* ability alone. Then go and be the same!

But maybe you're someone who gets a little nauseous reading these passages. The graphic violence disturbs you. Even though you might *know* in your head that these are good things God commands, it still doesn't sit well with you. It just makes you uncomfortable.

And in a way, it should. God says in Ezekiel 18:23, *"Have I any pleasure in the death of the wicked, declares the Lord God, and not rather that he should turn from his way and live?"*

This is a tension that Christians are called to live in. **God-ordained, justified violence needs to be both mourned *and* rejoiced in.**

## SCRIPTURE

Mark 15:16–20

## READ

Thorns pressed into the skull. Flesh torn from the whips. Spit and mocking. Stakes through hands and feet. Death by crucifixion.

**The Canaanites were receiving the penalty for their sins. Jesus was receiving the penalty for ours.**

Because of sin, violence *is* the answer.

**Jesus suffered violence for our hope.** Though we mourn the reason why, we rejoice at His victory over death.

**We as Christians are called to be subject to violence for His name's sake that others might be saved.** Though we mourn the evil in the world, we rejoice for our *"reward is great in heaven"* (Matthew 5:4, 10–12).

**We pray for our governments to justly carry out violence to curb evil.** After the flood, God makes it clear for *all humanity* that death is to be the penalty for murder (Genesis 9:5–6). God also makes it clear that it is *not* to be carried out in an anti-hero sort of vengeance (Romans 12:19–20). Instead, the government is to be a *"servant of God, an avenger who carries out God's wrath on the wrongdoer"* (Romans 13:1–7). We know God desires justice, so this should be done by due process with full confidence of the crime committed (Deuteronomy 17:6–13). And when governments carry this out unjustly, God *will* avenge them for their injustice.

**And the only way to finally extinguish unrepentant evil is through violence from God alone.** God will judge all who have chosen evil and assign them their just, physical, and psychological suffering (Matthew 25:30, Revelation 20:11–15). Though we will mourn for a little while those who have rejected Christ, we will be eternally rejoicing in His justice that has freed us from the reign of sin (Revelation 18:20, 21:4).

If you naturally rejoice over the destruction of evil, I'd encourage you to practice mourning for the souls of those who carry out evil. Be incredibly intentional at praying for and loving your "enemies" well that they may be saved. Pray that they would become powerful testimonies of Christ's love. Pray for your own heart that you might genuinely love those who hate God. Pray that you would have a heart like Christ's that takes no joy in the death of the wicked person.

If you naturally mourn for the hearts of evil people, practice praying for justice to be carried out so that it might awaken them to Christ. Pray for the victims of their evil. Pray for those with the power to carry out justice to do so effectively and safely. Pray for your own heart that you might not unwisely allow evil to continue simply for the sake of "mercy." Ask the Lord to grant you *His* perspective on evil so that you can properly identify it and may genuinely rejoice when justice is carried out.

Wrestling with this tension is good. It is part of the process of shaping us into Christ's likeness.

## JOURNAL

**Joshua 10:14 says that** *"the LORD fought for Israel."* When was a time you knew God was fighting for you? How can you see Him fighting for you now? (Think both circumstantially and within you!)

**Christians are called to mourn like God does over evil.** Do you mourn like Him? Does the suffering of others affect you? How? Have you grown callous to evil? Do you take time to pray on behalf of the oppressed? Do you pray for godly justice to be carried out?

**Christians are called to rejoice when God's justice is carried out.** Does injustice infuriate you? Does the wrongdoing of others charge you toward action? Do you rejoice when darkness is exposed and curbed? Do you seek to carry out justice within your spheres of influence? Do you consistently and fairly apply justice? Do you pray for your "enemies" that they might come to know Jesus?

## CLOSING PRAYER

*"Lord Jesus, please make me more like You. You are more heartbroken over evil than I ever will be. And You are more furious over evil than I ever will be. Lead me to become a person of great mercy and of great justice like You. I love You, Lord. Amen."*

# 58

# The Twelve Tribes

## OPENING PRAYER

*"Good Shepherd, You have led me here today. You have orchestrated this time and place for me to abide with You in Your Word. Please do a mighty work in me. In Your name, Jesus, amen."*

## SCRIPTURE

Joshua 13:1–7

## THINK

- *Where is His grace?*
- *Where is His lordship?*

## READ

Joshua is getting a bit too old for war. Some estimate that it took anywhere between five to seven years to conquer the cities up until this point. He's had incredible victories, but it's time to pass the torch.

In the meantime, God tells him to divide the land as an inheritance to the tribes. All the tribes have to do is continue the conquest, faithfully trusting God as they had been this whole time (with the exceptions we've explored already).

What follows in chapters 14 through 21 are the borders that each of the tribes are to inherit. Joshua 13 highlights the land Moses gave to three of the tribes, and Joshua 14:1–2 tells us that the rest were determined by lot. In other words, they would do something like rolling dice to allow God to sovereignly determine who would get what land. This would prevent the peoples from suspecting favoritism by Joshua and the leaders overseeing this process. What a wise God He is!

We won't look in depth at all of these land boundaries, but I do want to spend some time getting familiar with each of the tribes of Israel. Knowing their origins and keeping track of when they show up in Scripture will help us pick up on themes, patterns, and storylines we might've missed otherwise.

It may seem monotonous at first glance, but *so many* things are going on! **And the more understanding we have of the finer details, the more depth our experience reading Scripture will have. The more depth we have, the more awe we have of God. And the more awe we have of Him, the more love we will have of Him.**

I recommend looking up a map of the twelve tribes during the time of Joshua, to have it as a reference while reading this chapter. When looking at it, what questions arise? (We might answer some of them here!)

As a reminder, the twelve tribes originated from the twelve sons of Jacob. However, though they are often referred to as the twelve tribes, there are actually thirteen! (Kind of...you'll see.)

Let's take a look at these tribes, going from the oldest to the youngest...

**1. Reuben.** He's the firstborn of Jacob, son of Leah, and the one who persuades his brothers not to kill Joseph in Genesis 37. He forfeits his firstborn privilege, however, after having an affair with one of his "stepmoms," Bilhah (Genesis 35:22, 49:3–4). Yeah...messed up. No significant hero of Israel will arise from this tribe, and they were given some of the land east of the Jordan as Moses had promised.

**2. Simeon.** He's the second oldest, also a son of Leah, and the brother who was held in captivity in Egypt by Joseph for a period of time (Genesis 42). In Genesis 34 (a story we didn't cover and one that's not quite suitable for younger audiences), he and Levi massacre a village. As a result, his tribe's inheritance will be be disperesed, which is why they were merely given cities spread throughout Judah's territory (Genesis 49:5–7).

**3. Levi.** Meet the third son of Leah whose descendants would be chosen by God to work for the priests. Like the Simeonites, they were not to be given land as a consequence of the original Levi's violence with Simeon (Genesis 49:5–7). Instead, *"the LORD God of Israel is their inheritance"* (Joshua 13:33), indicating that they will be receiving their blessing and security directly in relation to their work with the priests (who were also Levites). Rather than a region of land, they would be assigned cities and plots of land throughout Israel as a whole (Joshua 21). This is why there is no land of Levi on the map you are looking at. I personally think God was intentional with this, wanting His "holy" tribe to be spread among the people as a testimony and consistent reminder to follow Him!

**4. Judah.** It will be Jacob's fourth son of Leah that will bear the royal line of Christ, which Jacob prophesies in Genesis 49:8–12. (Remember how Leah was the unloved wife? Look at the incredible honor God gives her! So kind!) Judah was the largest tribe while they wandered through the wilderness (likely highlighting God's blessing over them) and marched in front of everyone else as they made their way, indicating their military strength (Numbers 1:26–27, 2:9). In Joshua 15, they will be allotted the greatest amount of land and will play a very prominent role in future stories.

**5. Dan.** Hopefully you recall that Jacob's second wife, Rachel, was unable to have kids at first. So, like her grandma Sarah before her, she tells Jacob to sleep with her servant, Bilhah, in Genesis 30. (This is the same servant Reuben will sleep with...yeah, so bad.) Bilhah first gives birth to Dan, who'll get a smaller plot of land located near the coast. This tribe is going to do some pretty awful things, so keep an eye out for it!

**6. Naphtali.** Here we have Jacob's second son with Bilhah (Genesis 30). Another smaller tribe, Naphtali will appear in some prophecies later on. Jesus will do much of His ministry in this tribe's land, as it borders the Sea of Galilee.

**7. Gad.** In response to Rachel giving Bilhah to Jacob, Leah gives *her* servant Zilpah to Jacob, who will first give birth to Gad (Genesis 30). They are another smaller tribe that settles on the east side of the Jordan as promised by Moses. They are certainly one of the more "background" tribes compared to others.

**8. Asher.** The second son that Zilpah bears for Jacob (Genesis 30), Asher is to inherit one of the northernmost coastal regions of the Promised Land. They're also a minor player in the events that unfold, but it's good to know who they are.

**9. Issachar.** In Genesis 30, Leah bears a fifth son for Jacob. Like Gad and Asher, Issachar is another more obscure tribe who will appear from time to time in the narrative.

**10. Zebulun.** Like the few brothers listed before, Leah's sixth and final son will not make too much of an impact on the main biblical storyline, save a prophecy about the tribe's territory that Jesus will fulfill (Isaiah 9:1).

**11. Joseph.** This is where it gets a little confusing. You might've noticed on your map that Joseph doesn't have a region assigned to him. Hopefully you recall that Joseph was Jacob's favorite son of his favorite wife, Rachel (Genesis 30). As we read, he gets sold into slavery but eventually becomes the second-in-command of Egypt. During this time, he marries an Egyptian woman and has two sons, Manasseh and Ephraim (Genesis 41:50–52). Then in Genesis 48, Jacob declares that these two boys will be counted as his sons. So sometimes you'll see the tribes listed separately or as one "tribe of Joseph."

> **11a. Manasseh.** This tribe is sometimes referred to as the "half-tribe" of Manasseh because, well, they split in half. Some decided to take residence on the east side of the Jordan along with Gad and Reuben, while the rest took the designated areas by lot (though they pushed Joshua for more in Joshua 17).

> **11b. Ephraim.** Though Ephraim is Joseph's second son, Jacob gives him the honor of being the firstborn (Genesis 48). This is the tribe that Joshua comes from and will play an important (albeit tragic and evil) role in future stories.

**12. Benjamin.** In Genesis 35, Rachel gives birth to Benjamin and tragically dies in the process. He is the youngest of the twelve sons and the one Joseph asks to see in order to test his brothers (Genesis 42–44). Benjamin will be the smallest of the twelve tribes but will produce some of the most famous people in the Bible, both good and bad.

## SCRIPTURE

John 14:1–7

## READ

Each of these twelve tribes will play roles in the story of God, some more prominent than others. And yet God's desire was that each of them have a place to belong within His plan.

**God had been preparing an earthly inheritance for the Israelites. He is currently preparing a heavenly inheritance for you.**

What hope we have!

**The inheritance of the Israelites was guaranteed if they continued to fight for it. Our inheritance is guaranteed because Jesus fought for us!**

Praise Jesus, for a mighty God He is!

## JOURNAL

**Like He did for the Israelites, God has promised an eternal land for you and has called you to be faithful in the meantime.** How is that comforting? Challenging? How might you heed Jesus' command to not let your heart be troubled in light of what He is doing for you in Heaven right now? Consider how specific God was with the territories of the conquest. How specific do you think Jesus is going to be with your "place" in the New Heaven and New Earth?

**Some of these tribes will be major players in God's story while others will be more in the background, but Jesus is still the main character.** Do you feel like a major player in God's story? A minor character? A background character? Not even part of it? How might the story of these tribes encourage you? Do you consider Jesus the main character of your life? How would your life change if you did?

**In some parts of the Bible, it can be difficult to find beauty because they appear at first glance to just be a long list of details.** But God included these details for a reason. Not just for the people back then, but for *you*! So one of the best things you can do when you come across these passages is to foster a heart of curiosity. Practice asking lots of questions and then seeking answers to those questions. If you would like to try with an easier "dry" part of Scripture, read Joshua 16–17. In the back of this book, I've provided a list of great questions to ask to get your curiosity going. Then come up with your own as you go! (I highly recommend trying this with a friend!)

## CLOSING PRAYER

*"Lord, all of Your Word is profitable for teaching, reproof, correction, and training in righteousness, including the parts that are challenging to get through right now. May those challenging parts of Scripture become some of the most life-giving parts for me. May I love Your Word more and more each day. In Your name, Jesus, amen."*

# 59

# Caleb's Rest

## OPENING PRAYER

*"Lord Jesus, may my heart be open to You during this time. Please strengthen and embolden me to follow You in all things. May I rejoice in obedience unto You! I love You, Jesus. Amen."*

## SCRIPTURE

Joshua 14:6–15

## THINK

- *Where is His grace?*
- *Where is His lordship?*
- *How would you describe Caleb's character?*

## READ

*Forty-five years of waiting.*

He had been courageous and full of faith. There was nothing God couldn't do! And his faith remained just as vibrant all those years.

*Forty-five years of waiting.*

Despite his faithfulness, he was forced to live in the wilderness with his unfaithful generation for decades. Yet his trust in God remained.

*Forty-five years of waiting.*

God through Moses promised him a piece of that land back in Numbers 14:24. He had not forgotten that promise from God.

*Forty-five years of waiting.*

*"And there we saw the Nephilim [the Anakim]...and we seemed to ourselves like grasshoppers,"* his compatriots had cried (Numbers 13:33). By God's grace, he would slay those giants.

*Forty-five years of waiting.*

And he would see God's faithfulness. Caleb is given the land of Hebron. It's where Abraham, Sarah, Isaac, Rebekah, Jacob, and Leah had all been buried as they awaited God to fulfill His promises to them.

I can only imagine the tears he shed in wondrous joy when he could finally rest...

## SCRIPTURE

Hebrews 3:7–4:13

## READ

Caleb and Joshua were prefigures of the coming Holy Spirit proclaiming the good news of Jesus. *"Here's the promise! We can take it! All you have to do is have faith in God!"* And like their generation, so many today harden their hearts against this invitation and choose to rebel.

Caleb's generation died in the wilderness unable to enter an earthly rest. Many in our generation will die on earth unable to enter Christ's heavenly rest.

Israel had been in the wilderness, in between freedom from the slavery of Egypt and the obtainment of the Promised Land. You and I are in the wilderness now, in between freedom from the slavery of sin and the obtainment of the New Heaven and New Earth.

If you are in Christ, you haven't hardened your heart. But now you are like Caleb living in the midst of a harsh and unbelieving world. (Fortunately, Christ has given us many "Joshuas" to walk alongside us!)

We are called to live like Caleb, courageous and full of faith. Unrelenting and striving to enter the rest of Christ's "Promised Land."

We are to *"exhort one another every day"* so that we won't *"be hardened by the deceitfulness of sin."*

We are to fight the giants of our flesh that we may remain faithful. We are to abide in the *"sword of the Spirit,"* the Word of God that is *"sharper than any two-edged sword"* to destroy the lies and deceptions of Satan.

I can only imagine the tears we will shed in wondrous joy when we finally enter Christ's rest...

## JOURNAL

**Forty-five years of waiting.** Are you in a season of waiting? How do you think Caleb was able to *grow* in his faith all those years? How did he wait well? How does our Hebrews passage here show us how to wait well? What would the day-to-day look like? What would your mindset be? What would you be like when that season of waiting is over? Have you been waiting well?

**Forty-five years of waiting.** What would it look like to wait poorly? What would the day-to-day look like? What would your mindset be? What would you be like when that season of waiting is over? Have you been waiting poorly?

**Forty-five years of waiting.** If you are in Christ, *you are by default waiting* for final rest in Him, be it through death or in His return. Have you been waiting well? Have you been waiting poorly? Are you conscientiously waiting at all? Since you don't know when you will die or when He will return, how must that affect your urgency to wait well?

## CLOSING PRAYER

*"Lord Jesus, may I practice waiting well, both in the seasons I find myself in and in this place between slavery and ultimate freedom. May I be a person of exhortation for others to wait well. Please Jesus, may You be glorified in how I wait. Amen."*

60

# Joshua's Farewell

## OPENING PRAYER

*"Jesus, may my longing for You increase. May my hunger for You abound. May my thirst for You be overwhelming. Please, Lord. Help me not leave this time without tasting Your goodness once again. Amen."*

## SCRIPTURE

Joshua 1:1–9
Joshua 23–24

## THINK

- *Where is His grace?*
- *Where is His lordship?*
- *What work has God done in Joshua?*

## READ

*"Be strong and courageous. Do not be frightened, and do not be dismayed, for the LORD your God is with you wherever you go."*

These words were repeated over and over again to Joshua. And now he was repeating them to the next generation. Why?

Because after 110 years of seeing God at work, he knew it was true.

It's as if he's saying, *"I've seen this. I've lived this. Now go live with Him the same way."*

**Because he's lived it,** he knows for certain that God always keeps His promises.

**Because he's lived it,** he knows for certain that God is with him.

**Because he's lived it,** he knows for certain that God will never leave or forsake him.

**Because he's lived it,** he knows for certain that fear and dismay truly have no place in his life.

**Because he's lived it,** he knows for certain that keeping and doing all that God has written always leads to a prosperous way and good success.

**Because he's lived it,** he knows for certain that no matter what everyone else decides to do, he and his house will serve the Lord.

Joshua was able to experience God this way because he consistently loved and obeyed Him over a long period of time. Imperfectly, but consistently. And so God was able to reinforce and strengthen Joshua's conviction over the years by *His* own consistent faithfulness. May it be so for us!

## SCRIPTURE

2 Timothy 4:1–8

## READ

Paul passes the torch to Timothy and the next generation of Christians. He knows what they will go through, like Joshua did. The temptations, the deceptions, the spiritual warfare, the lures of a worldly culture...

And like Joshua, Paul exhorts Timothy to live as he lived. To preach the Word, meaning he really has to *know* it, not wavering to the right or to the left from it.

To *"be strong and courageous"* so that he *can* preach into cultures that reject Jesus.

To believe that, despite suffering, clinging to Christ the Word will produce the greatest prosperity and success in the New Heaven and New Earth.

And it's within that context that Paul wants Timothy to remember that the fight *will* cease. The race *will* end. The faith *will* be made sight. Christ *will* return to judge the living and the dead. And He *will* give a crown of righteousness to those who have loved His appearing.

The question for both Timothy and the Israelites is whether they will continue to fight or not. Will they continue to run the race? Will they continue to keep the faith?

Soon they would not be able to rely on Paul or Joshua, which is a good thing. It forces them to rely on Christ even more fully than they ever have before. **And if they choose faithfulness, they'll live in the certainty of Christ.**

## JOURNAL

**"Because you've lived it, you know for certain that..."** How would you finish this sentence? How would you like to finish this sentence? What would it take for you to truly finish that sentence?

*"Choose this day whom you will serve."* What is important about the word *"choose"* here? What is important about the words *"this day"*? Why is Joshua using the word *"serve"*? Whom have you been choosing to serve? What would it mean to choose Christ today? How does waffling back and forth between Christ and other things hinder our faith? What might it reveal?

**Joshua spends time recounting their history with God so far.** Why was it important for him to do that? How would you recount *your* history with Jesus to the next generation? What is your family's history with Jesus? How might that encourage you? Remember, you are part of the church...how might remembering the history of the church encourage your faith?

## CLOSING PRAYER

*"Father, create in me a deep consistency with You, exponentially more than I have now. I want to know Your certainty. May You be praised and glorified in my life. Amen."*

Every word of the Bible was given to us by God in order for us to know Him, this story, and how to live with Him within this story. The Bible is the very Word of God.

Alongside this truth, the Bible was written by humans. God didn't write down some words on a scroll and hand them to His followers. He didn't "possess" or control the writers in some sort of trance. No, He instead empowered and used various people to write these words and put them together over the course of many, many years. These words were most likely prayed over and selected carefully as they were being written.

This may freak us out and cause us to doubt the trustworthiness of the Bible, but it doesn't need to. This mysterious reality of God using ordinary people to accomplish His purposes is prevalent in Scripture. And think about it this way: If we truly believe Jesus is both fully man and fully God, we can truly believe that the Bible is both fully written by humans and fully "written" by God.

I bring this up not only to encourage trust in the Bible, but also because the "human-ness" aspect of Scripture affects how we are meant to read the Bible. Scripture is written in various ways and genres to inform us how to engage with it. Let's see how it's organized...

## How It's Organized

The Bible is split into two parts that we call the Old and New Testaments. A more accurate term might be Old and New "Covenants" that God makes with His people. Let's look briefly at each....

### *The Old Testament*

The Old Testament consists of 39 books (originally scrolls) written by various prophets, kings, and scribes over the course of about 1,500 years. This is the "Bible" that Jesus and His followers would be familiar with while He was doing ministry on earth.

We call it a "testament" or "covenant" based largely around the promised relationship God makes with Israel during this period of history. (You can think of covenant as a divine agreement between two parties.) These 39 books are organized in our Bible today by genre:

> **Narrative:** Genesis, Exodus, Leviticus, Numbers, Deuteronomy *(these five are called the Torah or Pentateuch),* Joshua, Judges, Ruth, 1 & 2 Samuel, 1 & 2 Kings, 1 & 2 Chronicles, Ezra, Nehemiah, Esther

> **Writings:** Job, Psalms, Proverbs, Ecclesiastes, Song of Songs (or Song of Solomon), Lamentations

> **Prophecy:** Isaiah, Jeremiah, Ezekiel, Daniel, Hosea, Joel, Amos, Obadiah, Jonah, Micah, Nahum, Habakkuk, Zephaniah, Haggai, Zechariah, Malachi

**Narrative**, sometimes called "Historical," focuses on storytelling. It primarily reveals who God is by His actions and interactions with people. While all stories are *descriptive* of things that happen, not everything is *prescriptive.* This means that some things God commands are meant only for certain individuals or groups for a certain time and not necessarily for us, the modern-day reader.

For example, at one point God asks Abraham to sacrifice his son. (Spoiler alert: God stops him at the last moment.) This is God giving a command to Abraham *only*. Not to us.

It also means that people will do things of their own agency that God doesn't necessarily approve of. In fact, most people in the Old Testament will do terrible things regularly. These stories aren't there inviting us to imitate everything they do. Instead, they simply tell us what happened, and we have to use context to understand God's perspective of their actions.

**Writings** can be described as poetry and wisdom literature. They show us how we can engage with God, how others have engaged with God, and wisdom on how to live in light of who God is. Most of them are highly personal so that we can relate to them and use them as a framework in how we can connect with God. They will often contain metaphors to reveal truths God wants to communicate with us.

**Prophecy** focuses on words spoken by God through prophets to people going through a particular situation. They share God's perspective on the current events of the time and sometimes glimpses into the immediate, distant, and *distant* distant future (sometimes all at once!). They're typically warnings, judgments on evil, calls to repentance, comfort in hope, and foreshadowings of Jesus coming to redeem all things. These books have A LOT of imagery and can often say many things at the same time.

Most books will include multiple genres within them. Exodus, which is primarily narrative, contains song and law subgenres. Daniel, which is primarily prophetic, contains narrative. Genesis has prophecies and genealogies, and so forth. It's important for us to distinguish between them so we can best understand how God is communicating.

## *The New Testament*

The New Testament consists of 27 books (also originally scrolls) written by various followers of Jesus over the course of about 50 years. They focus on Jesus fulfilling the promises of the "old covenant" and establishing a "new covenant" with His followers (aka a new way to engage with God in light of what He's done). Like the Old Testament, these books also have various genres:

> **Narrative:** Matthew, Mark, Luke, John *(these four are referred to as the Gospels)*, Acts

> **Epistles (aka Letters):** Romans, 1 & 2 Corinthians, Galatians, Ephesians, Philippians, Colossians, 1 & 2 Thessalonians, 1 & 2 Timothy, Titus, Philemon, Hebrews, James, 1 & 2 Peter, 1 & 2 & 3 John, Jude

> **Prophecy:** Revelation

The description above about the **Narrative** books of the Old Testament could largely be said about the New Testament ones listed here, though the focus is on the person of Jesus, His mission, and His establishing a new covenant with His people.

The **Epistles** are letters written by various followers of Jesus to different churches and individuals about how to follow Jesus in light of this new covenant. The writers are typically trying to address theological questions, church culture issues, and ways all Christians are to walk with the Holy Spirit.

The lone **Prophecy** book, Revelation, is similar to the prophecy books of the Old Testament, except that it serves as an epistle to God's people as well.

And like with the Old Testament books, you will also find subgenres within each of these books. For instance, Jesus will tell parables (made-up short stories) to communicate truths about His Kingdom.

## Bible Translations

It can be easy to forget that the Bible you're reading likely isn't in its original language. (If it is, that's very impressive and you probably don't need to read the rest of this.) The Old Testament was originally written in Hebrew with bits of Aramaic sprinkled in, while the New Testament was originally written in Greek.

Throughout history, incredible people have taken the time to translate the Bible into hundreds of languages so that people of all backgrounds can read God's Word for themselves.

So why are there so many English translations? Great question! One of the reasons has to do with the goals of the translators. This typically comes down to whether the translation should be more of a "word-for-word" translation or more of a "thought-for-thought" translation.

For instance, consider someone says, "Jack is a cool dude." You and I understand that "cool" doesn't refer to Jack's body temperature but that it suggests he has an air about him that people like, typically related to his sense style and the way he carries himself. But how should a translator communicate that?

A "word-for-word" translator might use the literal direct translation for the word "cool" in their language in order to be faithful to the original, running the risk of the reader misunderstanding its meaning. A "thought-for-thought" translator might pick a less accurate translation for "cool" so that the meaning comes across more easily, but it may distance the reader from the original words.

Or take the Greek word "adelphos" that is used in the Bible. Some translations simply translate this as "brothers" because the cultural understanding was that it referred to both men *and* women. Sort of like when people say, *"Hey, guys!"* We generally know that that can be referred to a group of men *and* women, even though it's a masculine term. But to not confuse some readers, some translations have translated "adelphos" as "brothers and sisters."

These are the decisions translators need to make in order to best serve the church. Referring to multiple translations of the Bible can be a very healthy practice to keep us from misunderstanding what God has said. If you're curious as to which translations are more "word-for-word" and which are more "thought-for-thought," I recommend doing a quick search online.

This study uses the English Standard Version (ESV), which is considered a more "word-for-word" translation.

## People

*Have I seen this name before?*
*Why are they mentioned?*
*What does their name mean?*
*Who are they related to?*
*What tribe are they from?*
*What's their ethnicity? Is that relevant?*
*If they're non-Jewish, how have his/her people interacted with the Jews?*
*Are they a man or woman? Is there significance there?*
*Who might've influenced them?*
*Is there a unique detail included about them? Why is this detail here?*
*What do these details say about that person?*
*How old were they during this moment?*
*What was the context in which they grew up?*
*What might their worldview be?*
*What has God said to them before?*
*Has anyone said something similar to what they are saying here?*
*Who was their dad? Their mom?*
*How might their parents have influenced him/her?*
*Are they repeating any mistakes others have made?*
*Are they redeeming any mistakes others have made?*
*How will their actions impact others?*
*How is faith/lack of faith being shown?*

## Locations

*Where have I seen this location before?*
*What does the location's name mean?*
*Has God done something here before?*
*Has someone else experienced something here?*
*Why would God include this detail?*
*Where is this actually located?*
*What kind of climate would this location have?*
*Is the location desirable for some reason?*
*How far away is it from where the action was taking place before?*
*How long would it take to travel there?*
*How would someone travel there?*
*Is this place safe or dangerous?*
*Who is the ruling government at this moment?*
*What is the culture like here?*

## Themes & Motifs

*Where have I seen this phrase before?*
*Is a direction being repeated? (North/South, Up/Down, Out/In, etc.)*
*Is this a foreshadowing of the gospel?*
*Is this a foreshadowing/reflection of Jesus in some way?*
*Is it related to God's presence?*
*Is it related to the Tabernacle/Temple?*
*Is there hope here?*
*Has someone or something been "set apart"?*
*Have I seen someone do something like this before?*
*How might this glorify God?*
*How might this dishonor God?*
*How does God display His love here?*
*Why would God want us to know this?*
*Why would God want the original/first readers to know this?*
*How does this reveal a character trait of God?*

## Greater Context

*What genre is this book of the Bible?*

*How does the genre inform how this should be read?*

*Does this passage have a unique subgenre?*

*Is this literal? Metaphorical? Explanatory of an experience?*

*Who is the author of this book?*

*What is the author's context?*

*What do we know about the author?*

*Why did the author write/include this?*

*Who likely comes to mind first as the author's main reader/hearer?*

*What has just happened in the story?*

*How have prior events impacted this passage?*

*How will this passage impact the following events?*

*Does Scripture refer to this passage/event at other times?*

*Does this event fulfill a prophecy? Foretell a prophecy?*

*What arguments are made prior to this passage?*

*How do the arguments inform the current train of thought?*

*How does this passage set up the next set of arguments?*

*What is the overall train of thought?*

## Items

*How might people feel looking at this item?*

*Is it a holy item?*

*Is this item supposed to be handled a certain way?*

*What is it made of? Why?*

*What technology was available at the time?*

*Is there an alternative item that would be used in this scenario?*

*Hey Laura*
*I know you know this*
*But so you hear it*
*I love you*